"Dave Mona's writing skills are verbally on display on University of Minnesota football radio pregame shows. He enriches the experience of every Gopher Fan who hears the broadcast and appreciates his keen insight beyond data and statistics. This award-winning storyteller has finally taken the suggestion of listeners and presented his insightful vignettes in written form."

—Dave Lee, WCCO Radio

"Huddle up with this book to relive these amazing stories from Dave Mona's unique perspective. If you've listened to Dave over the years, you already know he's a great storyteller—enjoy the best of the best!"

—Harvey Mackay, author of
Swim With the Sharks Without Being Eaten Alive

"With a father that was a well-known high school coach, Dave Mona got an early introduction to sports. He was an athlete himself, developed into a first-rate newspaper man, and then became CEO of a great public relations firm. A close personal friend, Dave has been a perfect partner on the *Sports Huddle* radio show and one of the great benefactors of the University of Minnesota."

—Sid Hartman, WCCO Radio and the *Star Tribune*

"*Beyond the Sports Huddle* epitomizes Dave Mona's love for all that is Minnesota. His pride in this state, its people, and its sports teams is awe-inspiring. His collection of stories will bring a smile to your face and warmth to your heart, and yes, we do all love one of Minnesota's greatest treasures—Sid Hartman! Go Gophers!"

—Coach Tim Brewster,
University of Minnesota Golden Gophers football team

"I was honored to preview *Beyond the Sports Huddle* while traveling on my many flights during March Madness. I found myself laughing out loud at many of Dave's Sidisms, tearing up over a personal story, and being amazed at others—like the one about the serial killer. Dave Mona captures Minnesota athletics from a perspective every Minnesota sports fan will enjoy. A must read!"

—Joel Maturi, Director of Athletics,
University of Minnesota

BEYOND THE SPORTS HUDDLE
MONA ON MINNESOTA

DAVE MONA

Voyageur Press

First published in 2008 by Voyageur Press, an imprint of MBI Publishing Company and the Quayside Publishing Group, 400 First Avenue N, Suite 300, Minneapolis, MN 55401 USA

Voyageur Press titles are also available at discounts in bulk quantity for industrial or sales-promotional use. For details write to Special Sales Manager at MBI Publishing Company, 400 First Avenue N, Suite 300, Minneapolis MN 55401 USA.

Library of Congress Cataloging-in-Publication Data

Mona, Dave.
  Beyond the Sports Huddle : Mona on Minnesota / Dave Mona.
    p. cm.
  ISBN 978-0-7603-3233-7 (hb w/ jkt)
  1. Mona, Dave. 2. Sportswriters—Minnesota—Biography. 3. Sportscasters—Minnesota—Biography. 4. Sports—Minnesota. I. Title.
  GV742.42.M65A3 2008
  070.4'497960922—dc22
  [B]

                                2008008617

Editor: Josh Leventhal
Designer: Helena Shimizu
Jacket design by John Barnett

Printed in the United States of America

Contents

Part II Making My Way in Journalism

Part III The Huddle, and Beyond

Introduction

For years I've been working with clients to help them develop their skills at storytelling. Most speakers are comfortable with facts, dates, and statistics, but research tells us that what people recall from speeches and conversations are the stories and anecdotes.

For more than two decades I've been speaking or emceeing events throughout the region. I've collected literally dozens of stories about some of the interesting characters I've had the privilege of knowing. I've had a chance to work alongside Sid Hartman, Dave Moore, Garrison Keillor, Calvin Griffith, Halsey Hall, Harmon Killebrew, Kirby Puckett, and dozens of others, both inside the world of sports and beyond.

"Have you ever thought to write down any of those stories you tell?" is a frequent question I get at those speaking opportunities.

Several years ago I developed my outline and started thinking about a title. A quick Google search told me that the title I had in mind, based on a Halsey Hall conversation, was free and clear. And so, for about three months, the working title of this book was *The Pluperfect Subjunctive and Other Tales*.

It's not that often that you can find people united on an issue. But in this case, everyone I shared the title with had the same reaction. They didn't get it and didn't think anyone else would either. Reluctantly, I scrapped that title, but held onto the story as it was one of Halsey's best.

When you write something like this, it's a subjective call as to what should be included and what can be omitted. If you are a friend and former colleague looking for your name in the index, and if you don't find it, stay tuned for the sequel, *Far Beyond the Sports Huddle*.

If you are involved in one of the stories in this book and have a different recollection of things, I refer you to something I read in a similar book many years ago:

"Everything in this book is either true or the way I remember it."

Enjoy!

Part I

Growing Up in Minneapolis

First Impressions

One of the easiest ways to make a name for yourself in kindergarten is to get hit by a car.

In my case, the bandages were far more impressive than the injuries, but the total package was enough to qualify me as a role model of sorts.

My head wrapped in a turban-like bandage, I was a walking, talking show-and-tell as to what can happen when you don't look both ways. I was put on display by the school nurse for other pupils in the early grades. My condition probably resulted in better pedestrian habits than any lecture or filmstrip.

My older sister and I had walked down the alley to East 38th Street. Directly across the street was Shogren's, the neighborhood source of nearly everything I craved: Hire's Root Beer, Nesbitt Orange, and Oh So Grape, all available in bottles for a mere nickel apiece.

My sister, in trade for my promise not to leave the store, needed a few minutes to run an errand to the drug store, a block away on Bloomington Avenue. Between the comic book section and an almost endless assortment of penny candy, I wouldn't find it difficult to spend anywhere between five minutes to an hour.

For some reason, I decided her time was up and that even a five-year-old could navigate the short distance to our house.

Dashing out from between parked cars, I ran directly into the side of a passing Buick. That's where the story gets a little fuzzy. Somehow the neighbors got word to my mother and someone carried me to our house. Our family doctor was summoned, and he pronounced the injuries as somewhat superficial. I had a broken nose, a mild concussion, and numerous cuts and bruises on my forehead. The bandages were gone within a week.

That was about as exciting as anything that ever happened in our neighborhood in those days.

There were fireworks at Powderhorn Park on the Fourth of July, and the Southside Picnic. Peterson Hardware, at the intersection of Bloomington Avenue and East 38th Street, had a seven-inch Philco television, and we could go there almost any part of the day and watch test pattern.

My parents were both schoolteachers, so part of my daycare routinely was assigned to my Norwegian-born grandmother, who lived upstairs in our duplex. That arrangement ended soon after the time she encouraged me to incorporate into my nightly prayers the wish that my mother would give up her filthy habit of smoking cigarettes.

My grandfather was an evangelistic Lutheran minister who worked a five-state area preaching about the sins of drinking, swearing, smoking, dancing, and dating Roman Catholics—not necessarily in that order. My father had been on a ten-year probationary period with the church for marrying a woman who worked and smoked. His cause was not aided by the fact that he played a baseball game on the Sabbath and took a one-hop pitch in the throat while playing the unfamiliar position of catcher. Turns out he picked a bad day to experiment with chewing tobacco.

My father seldom talked about playing sports. He received plenty of attention as the basketball coach at Minneapolis South High School for some thirty-five years. I never knew that he'd excelled at sports until he was inducted into the Augsburg College Sports Hall of Fame, as a basketball player and a baseball player, in 1974. I learned at the induction ceremonies that he had once led his team in scoring against

My father, Luther Mona, (center, holding basketball)
with the Augsburg College basketball team, 1929

the Harlem Globetrotters. After his death in 1985, someone mailed me an old newspaper clipping about the time my father and Halsey Hall had officiated "a perfectly called" college basketball game.

We built our own house near the Hiawatha Golf Course in South Minneapolis in 1950. It was a great location. Each summer morning I would spend time wading in the portion of Minnehaha Creek that wound through the back nine of the golf course. We'd pull balls out of the creek and sell them back to golfers at ten balls for one dollar. It was better money than I was to make several years later as a bagger at the neighborhood Red Owl.

The best part of the summer was organized baseball. Our neighborhood team was the 42nd Street Merchants, and we proudly wore the names of the local businesses on our backs. After the organizing meeting each year, we would get on our bikes to make the call for the fifteen-dollar annual sponsorship. The fastest biker got to wear Scott's Drug Store, which always said yes each year. The Lake Inn was almost as easy. The slowest or laziest player got stuck with Lois Dry Goods.

We played in an eight-team league, and we would ride our bikes to play the role of visiting team at such exotic places as Nokomis Park, Minnehaha Falls, and Longfellow Park. Our home was Sibley Field, about a mile from our house. Playing in those summer leagues introduced us to dozens of kids our age who would later become teammates when a dozen elementary schools melded into three junior highs (Folwell, Nokomis, and Sanford) and two high schools (Roosevelt and South).

Riding bikes was the main way everyone got around. Whenever the White Castle put a coupon in the newspaper, my parents thought nothing of sending me on my bike to pick up one or two bags of the gourmet delights from the store at Hiawatha Avenue and Lake Street, about three miles from our house. I rode my bike everywhere in South Minneapolis, without ever owning a lock, and thought nothing of hitchhiking down 50th Street to caddy at faraway Edina Country Club. Several years later, when Metropolitan Stadium opened in Bloomington, I hitchhiked from Cedar Avenue and East 42nd Street to and from the new ballpark. It was easier to get a ride home with the departing crowd than it was to get a ride there, because we had to arrive two hours before game time to make the popcorn we would later sell. There was no extra compensation for making it. The highlight of my rides home was the time Orlando Cepeda, the Minneapolis Millers' best hitter, stopped to give me a ride. It was the first of many times in my life I wished I had spoken Spanish.

School boundaries changed before I entered fifth grade, and I was assigned to the recently expanded John Ericsson Elementary School. Our teacher, Eva Vinton, was a wonderful woman only a year or two from retirement age. After she left teaching, she grew bored with retirement and was featured in *The Minneapolis Tribune* as one of the oldest volunteers in the newly formed Peace Corps. I wasn't surprised.

My fondest memory of her happened near the end of the first week of school. It was recess, and a big fight broke out on the playground. I had a lousy view of the action and worked my way through the crowd to see what was happening. Just as I made it to the front row, the combatants lost interest and the fight ended as quickly as it began.

It turns out that Mrs. Vinton had seen the entire action from her third-story window.

"I'm a little ashamed of you," she told the class later. "All of you know better than to encourage fighting on the playground, but it was up to David, the new boy, to step forward and break things up."

It was my most dubious school achievement since the turban caper following my accident back in kindergarten.

To Look Sharp

Probably the first sporting events I ever saw on television were boxing matches. Every Friday night we'd sit in front of our Zenith and watch the action in faraway Madison Square Garden.

Over the years I'm sure I saw the likes of Rocky Marciano, Sugar Ray Robinson, Archie Moore, Floyd Patterson, Willie Pep, Kid Gavilan, Sandy Saddler, and Carmen Basilio. I have little to no recollection of who fought whom or who won.

What I do recall, with absolute clarity, is the show's opening: "The Gillette Cavalcade of Sports is on the Air." Before I had time to wonder just what a cavalcade was, the music would start:

To look sharp every time you shave

To feel sharp and be on the ball

To be sharp use Gillette Blue Blades

For the quickest, slickest shave of all!

I can remember little from going to school at the time. I've long since forgotten the exports of Peru, the capital of Ceylon (in its pre-Sri Lanka days), or how to find the square root of anything. But this I know for sure.

You'll wonder where the yellow went when you brush your teeth with Pepsodent.

Brylcream, a little dab'll do ya.

Old Spice means quality, said the captain to the bosun.

"What'll you have?" Pabst Blue Ribbon.

You get a lot to like with a Marlboro.

Brusha, Brusha, Brusha. New Ipana toothpaste.

From the Land of Sky Blue Waters comes the beer refreshing.

Plop, Plop, Fizz, Fizz. Oh, what a relief it is.

Mmm, Mmm Good. That's what Campbell's Soups are.

Let's have another cup of coffee. Let's have a cup of Nescafé.

It's been years since I've heard any one of those jingles, but they leap instantly to mind as an occasional *Jeopardy* answer or when filling out a crossword puzzle. To wit:

24A: B. Brown's home. Four-letter word

Too easy once you've heard, "Hi, I'm Buster Brown. I live in a shoe."

We heard jingles so often, we had our own versions of many of them:

Pepsi Cola Hits the Spot

It Makes You Throw Up a Lot

Push a Button, Pull a Chain

There Goes Pepsi Down the Drain.

Many decades later, when I was working in public relations, I was in a meeting discussing how to build a reputation for a new product that was being introduced with heavy advertising support.

"Has anyone thought of a jingle?" I naively asked.

"Jingles don't work anymore," the ad agency guy offered,

making no attempt to hide his amusement at the suggestion. "Nobody's done them for years. The industry has moved beyond that stage."

He may have been right, but he never grew up knowing that when the weather ball was red, warmer weather was ahead.

Bat Boy of the Giants

I never met Garth Garreau. Never corresponded with him. And, above all, never thanked him for getting me through fourth grade.

And fifth grade.

And sixth.

You see, Garth Garreau was a novelist of sorts. He penned the immortal classic *Bat Boy of the Giants*. So impressed was I with this book that I did my first written book report on it as a fourth grader at Bancroft Elementary School in South Minneapolis.

I transferred to John Ericsson Elementary School for fifth grade. Already a true believer in amortizing one's efforts over a period of years, I upgraded the vocabulary a bit in that book report and submitted the revised version to my teacher, Mrs. Vinton, whose knowledge of baseball was, I'm sure, greatly enhanced by my pithy insights.

The next year, destined to be the last in which I could take credit for this modest tome, I opted for an oral report, thus reducing my cost of purchase to a mere 16.67 cents per year.

I was prepared to go for the literary home run the next year, but I chickened out when I had my doubts about how Garreau's credentials would stack up against the likes of George Orwell, Jack London, and Ray Bradbury.

I always thought that book reports in junior high lacked a certain validity in that the only book read by everyone at Folwell Junior

High that year was Grace Metalious' *Peyton Place*. To the best of my knowledge, no one ever gave a book report on *Peyton Place*, but we learned a lot more practical information from that book than we ever did from *Little House on the Prairie* or *Call of the Wild*.

One of the most underrated jobs in junior high was working in the trucks during paper drives. This was years before recycling, and neighbors awaited with great interest the dates of the school's annual newspaper collection drives. Minneapolis at the time had two successful newspapers, the morning *Tribune* and the afternoon *Star*. By the time the paper drives rolled around, most garages were full of neatly tied bundles of newspapers, and even the people who gave little or no treats at Halloween couldn't wait to clear out their basements and garages.

Each classroom had its own neatly stacked piles, and the rooms with the biggest pile in each grade won some wonderful treat, such as root beer barrels or malted milk balls. The overall champions would get gift certificates for free comics at Nile Drugs or admission to the Nile Theater, in addition to the food treats.

After the morning judging, someone had to break up the piles of newspapers and load them into waiting trucks. It was a great job, especially after the debut of *Playboy* magazine in December 1953. It was remarkable how few of those magazines ever left in the trucks.

Aaron to Zuverink

It was the first day of either third or fourth grade when the teacher struck a degree of terror into the hearts of her students.

"This year," she said, "we are going to learn long division."

To illustrate, she wrote what appeared to be some seemingly impossible problem on the blackboard. For the purpose of illustration, let's say it was to divide 188 by 550.

To me, it looked a whole lot like the number of hits Joe Adcock had last year divided by the number of his at-bats.

Hank Aaron's 1955 Topps baseball card

So this was long division. With a little help from my sister, Judy, five years my senior, I had been figuring out how to calculate batting averages for nearly two years, but no one ever told me it was long division. I just thought it was practical math.

Until I was seven I shared a bedroom with my older sister. She knew early in life that she was destined to become a teacher. Whatever she learned in school that day, I learned later that night.

When I was nine, I bought my first baseball cards, and I was hopelessly hooked. I read each one, front and back.

When we began studying U.S. geography, I was the only one in the class who could name all the cities in the Three-I (Illinois/Indiana/Iowa) League. When our studies expanded to Latin America, I had at least a working knowledge of Cuba and Mexico.

Thanks to the cartoons at the bottom of the baseball cards, I knew a lot of useless information, such as the fact that a high pop fly was a can of corn and that the wife of one of the players was a stripper.

Baseball cards littered the floor of my room. Not knowing better, I sorted them by team and position. I read the newspaper every day to spot changes in starting lineups. I traded with other collectors with no regard for future value. If I needed a Jose Valdevielso and had a spare Ted Williams, that was a fair trade. No one had ever heard of a rookie card, and price guides were decades in the future.

One night, feeling unusually resourceful, I retreated to my room with a plan. I was tired of being the unfair recipient of criticism about cards being strewn all over the house. I would show my family that I was no stranger to organization.

Eschewing *My Little Margie* and *The Adventures of Davy Crockett*, I spent upward of four hours alphabetizing my more than one thousand prized possessions.

George Zuverink's 1957 Topps baseball card

Proudly, I showed the neat stacks to my sister.

Something was amiss. I knew it from her unusual silence.

"What's the matter? What did I do wrong?"

"Usually," she explained, careful to let me down as easily as possible, "when people alphabetize things they do it by last name."

It took me weeks before I could face the project again, but I finally tackled it. For that offseason, at least, the cards sat safely in two Buster Brown shoeboxes, neatly arranged from Aaron to Zuverink.

French Baseball

It was the spring of 1959 and I was sitting in French class when the teacher, Larry Swadner, called my name and asked me to step into the hall.

Quickly my mind raced with all the possibilities. Had I failed to properly conjugate my verbs? Did he know I was secretly and silently chewing gum? Did he know that I was writing an article for the *Roosevelt Standard* when I was supposed to be answering the questions at the end of the chapter?

My classmates were as suspicious as I was as I gathered up my books and made my way to the door. This was highly unusual stuff in a class that rarely provided much excitement.

As we got to the hallway, Mr. Swadner surprised me when he said he needed my help. Isn't it supposed to be the other way around, I thought?

While we were reading, I had noticed that he was writing something, but that didn't seem unusual.

At this point I should mention that Mr. Swadner was not only the French teacher, he was also the sophomore baseball coach. As often as the spring weather permitted, we were having after-school baseball practices. Many times these consisted of throwing in the girls' gym, because the varsity team had the larger boys' gym. We had gotten outside maybe three or four times to actually take some swings and field grounders and fly balls.

Mr. Swadner showed me his notebook. It was filled with the names of the forty or so players who had tried out for the sophomore baseball team.

"I've got a problem," the coach said. "The equipment manager tells me we've got maybe twenty-four uniform sets at the most, and I've got more than forty names here. I haven't really had a chance to see you guys play, and I know you played with a lot of these guys in junior high and in park board ball. I don't want to make any mistakes, so I was wondering if you'd take a look at the list."

Hey, this was good stuff. The big time. This was President Eisenhower coming to his cabinet for advice. It seemed like the least I could do for my country and my school.

The first name I looked for was my own. I'll be honest. Advice has its price.

Satisfied that my name was on the list, I continued.

Dave Nelson, the first baseman and the best athlete in the school. A no-brainer.

Randy Bundy, who could hit 350-foot home runs in sixth grade. Of course.

Pat Cronin, a great fielding shortstop.

Frank Kleckner, who would become the state singles champion in tennis, was a lock at second base.

I had to give Mr. Swadner credit. There were about a dozen solid baseball players on the team, and he had them all. It was with the next dozen names that I had a problem.

I must have frowned.

"Is there something wrong?" he asked.

"You can't cut Roger Hauge," I told him, without fear or hesitation.

"Why not? We've got at least five guys who can pitch, and we need help in the field."

"It's not that. Hauge has a car. A *station wagon*. We need him."

The logic was not lost on Mr. Swadner, who knew that the team's budget for transportation that season was about sixty dollars. A player with a station wagon was a huge asset.

Hauge's parents owned McDevitt-Hauge, the largest local mortuary. A station wagon was critical to a funeral director, but it was an even bigger asset to a transportation-challenged sophomore baseball team.

An Untimely Call

Most sports seasons end with a loss. The best season on the best team I ever played on ended with a phone call.

Things started to come together when I entered Folwell Junior High School. Dick Kempter, who ran the physical education program, was a strong believer in after-school programs, and he especially liked basketball.

Folwell at the time sent about sixty percent of its students on to Roosevelt High School; thirty percent went to South High School, where my father was the head coach for thirty-five years; and the remaining ten percent went to either Central High School or a private school such as nearby Minnehaha Academy.

Less than a month after the start of classes, word got out that anyone interested in playing basketball should show up after school. I couldn't wait as I sat through my history and math and science classes.

Finally the school day was over, and it was time to head for the boys' gym. There must have been 150 of us who showed up that first day. The gym was divided into thirds, and we were randomly assigned to teams. Most of the time when we weren't playing, we watched games on the ninth-grade court. What I saw there quickly convinced me that my father was going to enjoy the coming years.

Eric Magdanz was already a dominant player. He was six feet three inches tall and the owner of a deadly fadeaway jump shot. At this level of play, he could score at will from up to fifteen feet from the basket. The winning team kept the floor in these scrimmages, and his team played virtually the entire afternoon.

When I got home from school that night, my father was already there.

"How'd basketball practice go?" he asked.

"There's a ninth grader there who's better than anyone you've had in all the years I've watched your teams, and he's going to be at South next year."

I went on to tell him about Magdanz. My father had some good teams over the years, but he never had any height. His centers rarely topped six-foot-two, and for several years he started nobody over six feet.

He quickly got in touch with Kempter, and Magdanz went on to become a three-year starter at South, almost immediately dominating the Minneapolis City Conference. In his senior year, the team lost to eventual state champion Wayzata in the Region Five finals. After graduating from South, Magdanz went on to star for the University of Minnesota, and he still shares the school's single-game scoring record with forty-two points.

I was so excited to tell my father about Magdanz that I nearly forgot to mention our seventh-grade class.

"What did you think of your class?" he asked.

"We've got some kids who can really shoot from outside, and we've got a kid who can dunk."

"Come on," he said with a laugh. Nobody could dunk in those days. "How big is this kid?"

"Just about five-foot-eleven, maybe almost six feet, but you have to see him jump."

I was describing Dave Nelson, who went on to start at point guard for three years at Minneapolis Roosevelt. The kids who could shoot from the outside were Bill Bowman and Uldis Jansons, who became starters at the wing positions for Roosevelt. Anything that Nelson, Bowman, and Jansons missed usually wound up in the hands of Lenny Bjeldanes, who went on to be one of the two Roosevelt starters in Wayne Courtney's double-post offense, and who possessed a deadly turnaround jump shot from the high and low post.

From seventh grade on, we played basketball together about three hundred days a year. Unless the temperature was below zero, we played virtually every night at Sibley Field. Nelson's house, on the corner of Longfellow Avenue and East 40th Street, overlooked the basketball court. I gladly walked the nine blocks to the field, often carrying a snow shovel in case I was the first to arrive.

There was virtually no competition against other schools at the junior high level, but we more than held our own against older players, Magdanz included, in games played to twenty-one baskets under the lights at Sibley.

All the Folwell basketball players went on to Roosevelt, where we were joined by roughly equal numbers of kids from Nokomis and Sanford junior high schools. Roosevelt had won the state championship in both 1956 and 1957, and many of its stars came from Kempter's Folwell program. Kempter, always a good promoter, had done a good job in letting Courtney know that his incoming tenth-grade class had promise.

Before the first day of sophomore basketball, Nelson was already running with the varsity. Those of us left to play for sophomore coach Ralph Blake, also my homeroom teacher, could shoot, but we averaged just under six feet tall. We needed help on the boards, and the answer arrived when Fred Warn walked through the door.

None of us had ever seen or heard of Fred before, but he got our attention right away. He and his brother, David, and sister, Daisy, represented one hundred percent of the black population at Roosevelt.

Fred was a little over six-foot-three. He had played little organized basketball and had absolutely no shooting touch, but he could block any shot launched in his neighborhood, and he absolutely owned the backboards. Coaches Courtney and Blake had him work for hours on tip-in drills and rebounding exercises in which a metal lid was placed over the basket.

Evening practices would end with us making the trip from the girls' gym past the lunchroom to the boys' gym, where the sophomores would play the varsity reserves. Warn was devastating as he put back missed shots and swatted away any layup attempt within reach.

Even without Nelson, we won the mythical sophomore city championship, often topping eighty points in four eight-minute quarters and without the aid of a three-point line. The Courtney offense was predicated on full-court pressure and shooting the ball. There was no twenty-four-second clock, and we wouldn't have been hindered by a fifteen-second clock.

Warn joined Nelson in the varsity starting lineup in our junior year, and Bowman and Jansons were the first two players off the bench. We barely missed winning the very competitive Minneapolis City Championship. I was the thirteenth man on a fifteen-man team, rarely making an appearance before the final thirty seconds of a rout.

There was one exception.

We were playing a good Minneapolis South team coached by my father. I was in my usual spot at the end of the bench checking out the Henry cheerleaders, who had already arrived at the Minneapolis Auditorium for the next game. There were eleven Minneapolis city schools in those days. Every Friday, five games were played at the auditorium. When we weren't playing, we were scouting. We got to know the opposing teams very well. As a deep reserve, I became something of an expert on opposing cheerleaders.

I was checking out North's Andrea Hricko (who has been a friend ever since) and Henry's Gail Dahlvang (whom I later dated in college) when I thought I heard my name called. I was sure I was mistaken, because it was still the first half of a close game, and I never went in before Bowman and Jim Elfstrom.

"Mona, get down here," Courtney yelled. I wondered whether he'd left something important in the locker room.

"You're going in for Bozonie at the next whistle," he said. He had to be kidding. Paul Bozonie was a senior co-captain. But Coach Courtney, who stood about five-foot-five and who terrified both his team and his opponents, was not one to joke.

Roosevelt High School basketball team, 1961. That's me, sitting in the middle of the second row.

There was less than a minute remaining in the half, and we had a three-point lead. My game plan was obvious. Play good defense. If the ball came my way, I'd dump it off to a teammate as quickly as possible. No missed shots. No turnovers. No harm, no foul.

Almost immediately, South missed a long jump shot and the hard rebound came in my direction. I got my hands on the ball just as South guard Jerry Newsom hit me full stride. Newsom, a compact six-foot-one, 210-pound athlete, started for three years as linebacker for the University of Minnesota, back in the days when Minneapolis City Conference athletes were regularly starring for Minnesota.

The foul clearly was on Newsom, and I was shooting one and one. What happened to my low-profile plan? I'd known Newsom a little bit for two years. As he helped me up, he laughed and said, "Don't screw up."

I looked at Courtney, and he was smiling as he conferred with his assistant, Ralph Blake. I looked over at the South bench, and my father was holding an index card in front of his mouth and trying hard to look disinterested. Somewhere in the crowd, my mother was thankful that Newsom had left me in good enough condition to shoot the free throw. I looked at the six people lined up on either side of the line and realized I knew all of them and could recite most of their phone numbers by heart.

I was terrified. I knew I didn't belong in the game at this important point. Usually about a seventy-five percent free-throw shooter,

I couldn't feel the ball in my hands. Numbly, I lofted the ball toward the rim. It bounced twice and finally fell out. The half ended seconds later.

Courtney's halftime rants were fabulous. He had a photographic memory for every mistake anyone had made. He remembered nothing that had gone well. I had always listened in a voyeuristic way as he made his way around the room

"Nelson, you call that defense you were playing? You look like Ned in the first reader out there." None of us had a clue who Ned in the first reader was, but it clearly wasn't intended as a compliment. "Bozonie, let us know when you feel the motivation to get your first rebound. Dale [the other starting Nelson], you're making Meyers look like he's all world. Are you going to let him go around you all night? Mona. Kid, you had your chance."

It didn't sound real promising for the second half.

In our senior season, we were picked to be one of the better teams in the Minneapolis City Conference, one of the contenders for the title, but nothing special.

Our first game was at DeLaSalle, the defending Catholic Schools State Champion. They never lost at home, and beat us that night 56-48.

We beat Minnehaha Academy, a very good Benilde team, and won the City Conference opener with a 63-49 victory over North, one of the teams picked to compete with us for the title.

Our next game was at Williams Arena. The Gophers were playing St. Mary's of California that night, and we were playing the preliminary game. Our opponent was the undefeated and defending state champion, Edgerton.

This team is to Minnesota high school history what Milan is to Indiana. Their victory the year before made Edgerton without a doubt the most popular and most remembered champion in Minnesota high school history.

Our game started at 5:30 p.m., and the stands were nearly full. Newspapers said it was perhaps the most anticipated prelim game in Gopher basketball history. It wasn't because Roosevelt was playing. The crowd was one hundred percent behind the defending champs and cheered their every basket, even in warmups.

We were ready.

"Boys," Courtney told us, "nobody in this building wants us to win this game. Nobody expects us to win this game. But you are a better basketball team, and we are going to win this game. Do you understand? Is there anybody here who does not understand that we are going to win this game?"

I never thought it was a sales job. I always thought that we honestly would win. The crowd was aggressively hostile. The big-city school was booed constantly. The Gopher cheerleaders, the band, and the fans were united and vocal in their support of Edgerton. It made sense. We had more people in our three-year school than they had in their town.

We won 66-58, and it wasn't that close. We played flawlessly and won the respect of the news media. The result of our game was covered on the evening sports more than the Gopher game that followed. Edgerton had finally lost a game, and fans wanted to know more about the team that had beaten them.

We went on to win three more nonconference games before resuming play in the city conference against Edison. I spent the entire season as the team's sixth man and made my only start in the Edison game, which we won 92-55.

We beat West by 39 and Washburn by 30. Our closest game was a 58-49 victory over a Henry team led by center Mel Northway, who went on to start two years for the Gophers. All five Roosevelt starters averaged in double figures. A newspaper reporter at the time could find no other year in which that had happened, at any school.

St. Paul Central, an excellent team that had breezed through the St. Paul conference, met us in the annual Twin Cities game at Hamline University. There were so many fans at the game that people sat cross-legged against the out-of-bounds lines on both sides. Fans had to lean out of the way to allow an inbound pass. We won 57-43.

We beat Vocational, North, and South to win our district. All five of our starters were named to the five-man All-District First team.

Moving on to Region Five play, we defeated Royalton 70-62 and Mound 62-55 to qualify for the state tournament. As we celebrated the victory over Mound, several of their players said something about having the last laugh. We brushed if off and prepared to move into the tournament at Williams Arena the next weekend.

The plan was for buses to arrive at the school on Wednesday morning to take us to our hotel. No one on our team had ever spent a night in a hotel room. Tournament play started on Thursday, and we were the co-favorites, along with a very good Duluth Central team led by Terry Kunze and Mel Anderson.

At the completion of practice on Tuesday, Coach Courtney called a brief team meeting.

"I don't think it's anything to worry about," he said, "but there is a question about the eligibility of a couple of our juniors. I'm sure everything will be fine. We'll see you in the morning."

Nobody was terribly upset. This was a senior team. The top ten players were all seniors. We could dress only twelve players in the district competition. John Totushek and Warren Scamp, juniors who would be co-captains the next year, had played in the final seconds of the Mound game. Neither had scored, fouled, or to the best of our knowledge, even touched the ball. Popular as they were to their teammates, they were not critical to the success of the team.

I had a hard time getting to sleep, but finally nodded off after Cedric Adams' ten o'clock news.

My alarm was set for six in the morning, but the phone rang a little after five. I answered. It was our equipment manager, Rog Mahre. (Seven years later, Rog was the best man in my wedding.)

"We're out," he said.

It didn't sound like a joke.

"What do you mean, 'We're out'?"

"I couldn't sleep and had the radio on when they broke in to say that the High School League met through the night and voted just before five to kick us out and send Royalton in our place."

"Why? What did we do?"

"They said that two of our guys played in a DeMolay tournament last summer. The guys from Mound knew about it and turned us in."

"But that's not fair. Our guys didn't even score. Coach only put them in to keep the score down. The game was already over."

"I'm only telling you what I heard. It's all over the radio."

And so it was. An appeal was turned down. First-period classes at school were canceled and homeroom was extended as students cried in hallways and went in search of more information from the dozens of reporters who descended on the school.

Royalton played poorly and was eliminated. The small town north of St. Cloud invited our entire team to its postseason basketball tournament and treated us like visiting royalty and apologized for their showing in the tournament.

"We just didn't feel like we belonged," they told us.

Duluth Central played brilliantly and won the state championship. We watched from the bench seats at Williams Arena. Many of us wore our Roosevelt letter jackets for the first-round games, but we quickly tired of the media attention and left the jackets at home for the later rounds. For years after, whenever two or more of us got together, the conversation quickly turned to how we would have done against Duluth Central. We all agreed that losing would have been preferable to not knowing.

Totushek went on to become an admiral in the United States Navy. Scamp became a successful Minneapolis dentist.

Courtney never took another team to the state tournament. Gopher coach John Kundla spoke at our postseason banquet. He told of watching us win over Edgerton and said, "Boys, you may live your entire lives and never deal with anything this disappointing. I only hope and pray you will be stronger because of it."

Courtney, who went on to serve many years as mayor of Edina, spoke to the Roosevelt students, assembled at a hastily called meeting the morning after the ruling. He called the actions a "tragedy" and a "gross over-interpretation" of a well-intended law.

Charles Beekman, who owned and operated Beek's Pizza, where the team met after each game, presented the team with a sportsmanship trophy that was by far the largest trophy any of us had ever seen. It was nearly five feet tall. It still holds a place of honor at our class reunions, which we've celebrated every five years since we graduated.

The High School League rules were amended shortly after the ruling. Under the new rules, the individuals and not the team would be punished. Not long after, the rules were changed again to actually encourage summer competition.

Dave Stead, for many years the executive director of the Minnesota State High School League, later told me that the league

Reunion of the Roosevelt High basketball team, 1991

invited several of its former heads to submit their memoirs. One of them wrote that he was proud of the accomplishments of the league, but he had a single regret and that was their ruling on the Roosevelt team in 1961.

It was a nice thought, but it did little to ease the pain from a bullet that none of us saw coming.

My Jordan Moment

I have trouble remembering more than one PIN number and my mother-in-law's birthday, but I can still diagram the special inbounds play we used en route to ending Edgerton's basketball winning streak more than forty years ago. Other moments, from nearly a half century ago, also stand out in my sports memory.

I awoke one night not too long ago from a dream in which I had virtually total recall of the start of a high school basketball game I played in during my sophomore year at Minneapolis Roosevelt. We were scheduled to play at Minneapolis West.

Because the game was to be played shortly after school let out, the entire team was dismissed from sixth-hour classes. We met in the boys' gym to pick up our bags, which held our shoes and uniforms. Coach Ralph Blake carefully counted out the travel money: forty cents to each of the twelve players and our student manager. That was 20 cents bus fare each way.

We made our way to the nearest corner to catch the bus that would take us to Lake Street. It was about 12 degrees below zero, and the coach checked to make sure each player was wearing his stocking cap before leaving school.

We waited for nearly twenty minutes at Cedar Avenue and Lake Street for the bus, which took us to Hennepin and Lake. After getting off at that intersection, we ran the four blocks to West High School and arrived there shortly after school had let out.

"Where have you been?" a worried Coach Blake asked. "The game is supposed to start in ten minutes."

Most of us were in various stages of frostbite, and I can remember having no feeling in my fingers as we hurried through about three minutes of layups before the whistle blew for us to line up for the opening tip-off.

I had never felt less ready for a game.

We won the opening jump. The point guard fired a pass to me on the right wing and I broke for the basket and put up a quick layup. I was amazed to see it go in.

After about three minutes, West took a time-out. We led 14-2, and I had twelve points on six-for-six shooting.

When play resumed I was double-teamed for perhaps the only time in my career, but the defensive move was unnecessary. As feeling returned to my fingers, my normal shooting touch returned along with it, and the Cowboys had little to fear.

The memory of that game still resonates clearly in my head. There is something about sports that defies the limits of recollection.

And I am not alone. I have interviewed golfers who can accurately recall every stroke of an entire round, complete with analysis of what they could have done better. Football players can tell you who threw a key block on a run that happened when Eisenhower was in the White House.

Even the legendary Ted Williams, who had countless moments of greatness in his Hall of Fame baseball career, could conjure the minutest detail from a relatively insignificant game.

In Ken Burns' *Baseball* documentary, actor/comedian Billy Crystal conveyed a story about meeting Williams, his boyhood hero, later in life. Crystal, still awestruck despite his being a well-established celebrity, awkwardly began to tell Williams about a Yankees–Red Sox doubleheader that his father took him to in 1957.

"I can remember that you came up in the final inning of the second game," Crystal was explaining to Williams. "Bobby Shantz was pitching for the Yankees. The tying run was on base and everyone was screaming and yelling. I wanted you to hit a home run so bad, and I'll never forget that you struck out."

Williams, listening intently, smiled ruefully and said, "Curve ball. Low and away."

Boxcar Learning

It was, upon reflection, the hottest place I've been in my entire life. Rumor had it that the temperature at the back of the boxcar, parked for days in summer sunshine, lingered in the vicinity of 125 degrees.

It was the summer of 1961, and at my parents' urging I had secured a job in the warehouse of the Minneapolis Public Schools. Five of us, all between the ages of eighteen and twenty, shared some connection with the school system, which had gotten us our interviews. The McClure brothers were sons of a school librarian, and both of my parents were teachers in the system.

Our summer job was to fill orders, mostly textbooks, from all the schools so that each classroom would be ready for the first day of school in September. It was a massive task; each day we counted, boxed, and moved books from storage shelves to the loading dock. We also stamped each book as property of the Minneapolis Board of Education. Sometimes, out of boredom, we stamped them upside down.

The early part of the summer consisted of filling orders from existing shelf inventory. The work was tedious, but the conditions weren't bad, and the pay was better than that of my previous summer jobs filling grocery sacks at the Red Owl on Cedar Avenue and Minnehaha Parkway or filling catalog orders at the main Sears store on East Lake Street.

In early July we got the word that the freight cars, filled with new books from the publishers, would be arriving in less than a week. Our job was to unload the books, sort them, and stamp them, thereby helping to advance some unknown third grader on a relentless march toward fourth grade.

It was about 8:15 in the morning when we slid open the door of one of the freight cars and found it literally filled with boxes, each of which weighed more than Kate Smith. We started by taking the boxes one at a time to a pallet. Within fifteen minutes we had moved perhaps thirty boxes some fifteen feet, and we were soaked with sweat.

I don't remember whose idea it was, but someone suggested that we form a line, with one person inside the car handing the boxes to the next person and on down the line to the pallets. Because of the heat, we rotated positions every fifteen minutes.

Three days and four boxcars later, we found ourselves having lunch with the men who worked in the warehouse year-round. Ordinarily they had nothing to do with us, but on this day they were particularly friendly.

"We saw you guys unloading the boxcars," one said. "You know, unloading boxcars is a two-and-a-half-day job."

"Not if you do it our way," I happily volunteered in words never uttered by Jimmy Hoffa or Tony Soprano. "If you all work together and rotate the guy inside the car, you can get the whole thing done in half a day."

"I don't think you understand," he interrupted. "We work here all year 'round, and unloading boxcars is a two-and-a-half-day job."

We did it our way the rest of the summer, and the chill in the relationship helped cool things at the back of those cars. Not one of us was invited back the next summer.

Part II

Making My Way in Journalism

He Wrote the Book

Mitchell V. Charnley was a legend in Murphy Hall long before I got there. He wrote the basic journalism textbook used at the University of Minnesota and most of the other journalism schools across the country.

Charnley was intolerant of spelling and grammatical errors. He liked factual errors even less. If you turned in a class assignment that referred to Northrop Auditorium as Northrup Auditorium, you received an F. It was a rather effective grading system, as students seldom made that error a second time.

He graded papers with a red pen. You knew when you got a paper back from him that the more red it had on it, the worse the grade would be.

He also was more than willing to discuss his editing with you. He invited you into his office to argue cases where you thought he might have been too harsh. I had plenty of arguments with him. My record was perfect. I never won once.

In my junior year he dinged me half a grade for using "presently" when I should have used "currently." That afternoon I was at his door, paper in hand.

"What can I do for you?" he said with a smile. "I assume I must have made some mistake on your paper."

"I think I've got you this time," I told him, my confidence overflowing. "You marked me down for using 'presently' instead of 'currently.'"

"So I did," he confirmed.

"Well," I persisted, "they mean the same thing. You can interchange them."

"And you of course looked this up before coming to my office. You probably have me on this one. Let's just take a look at the dictionary."

I knew from his tone that I was dead meat, and one look at his well-worn dictionary proved it.

"Currently" meant something that was happening in the here and now. "Presently" meant something that was about to happen, as in "He is expected presently."

Refusing to admit defeat, I was back several weeks later with a column I had written for the *Minnesota Daily* student newspaper. It was about a longtime friend, Ken Jacobson, who played on the third team for the Gopher football team.

I was proud of the story and submitted it to a national competition, where it won first prize in a Hearst competition for feature sportswriting among college newspapers. I submitted it to Charnley for a class assignment, and it came back to me with twenty-three red suggestions for improvement.

After graduating, I began writing for *The Minneapolis Tribune* in September 1965. I had my first bylined article a few days later and was proud that the editors had chosen to display it on page one.

Two days later I looked in my mail slot and recognized the return address on one envelope; it was written with a familiar red pen.

I opened the envelope to find my story, neatly pasted onto a sheet of yellow copy paper. Above it, Charnley had written in red, "Mona. Nice yarn. Still having some problems with syntax. Mitch."

A Different Point of View

Most of my best friends on the Gopher football team never got a chance to play in games. These were guys who were stars in Minneapolis and St. Paul high schools who were a step slower than the likes of Bobby Bell, Carl Eller, and Sandy Stephens.

Day after day I'd go to practice and watch them try to emulate the offense and defense of the next week's opponents. They took great pride in their work, but never made the traveling squad and played only in major blowouts, if ever.

Ken Jacobson, one of my best friends in early grade school and a high school opponent at Minneapolis Central, was the titular captain of the Gopher's practice cannon fodder.

The column I wrote on "Jake" and his teammates won first place nationally in the William Randolph Hearst college newspaper division and was the only attachment I made on my job application to The Minneapolis Tribune. *(I've often suspected that judges identified much better with fourth-string quarterbacks than with All-Americans.) The column, entitled "Jake and the Bombers," appeared in the* Minnesota Daily *in 1964.*

Someone once said that behind every great football team was a great bunch of reserves. What that person should have gone on to say was that behind the great reserves was probably a bunch of not quite so talented ragamuffins known variously as the "bombers," "meat squad," "hamburgers," or a wealth of other descriptive titles.

Spokesman for the present Gopher squad is likeable, good-looking Kenny Jacobson. Jake, as he is known to his teammates and coaches, is a rare combination of droll humor and unbounding confidence. An eight letter man in high school, his high school yearbook said of Jake," Football isn't the only place where you need a line."

Referred to by his teammates as one of the fastest Gophers, both on and off the field, Jake used his running skills in high school to be rated All-Minneapolis in both football and baseball.

Now a senior, the highest rank Jake has been able to attain was second team right halfback for several days last spring. Is he discouraged by his spot on the fifth team, described as the "orange aides" by Jake in referring to their practice jerseys?

"You can't let it get you down," he says. "Sure it's tough sitting there, but you've got to keep thinking that maybe someone will get hurt and the coach will look down the bench and point to you. You always have to keep thinking that maybe next week will be the week."

Burger Coach "Smoky" Joe Salem speaks of Jake in high regard. "The personnel of the bombers may change from week to week," he said yesterday, "but Jake's our leader. He inspires the rest of the guys with his huddle humor and really drives his team."

The principal job of the bombers is to simulate the offense of the upcoming opponent against the first team defense. "On Monday and

Tuesday," Jake says, "we can sometimes move the ball past them." But by Wednesday and Thursday, they know what we're going to do better than we do.

"Sometimes it gets pretty frustrating. Like on a Thursday when they stop us fifteen consecutive times for no gain and [Assistant Coach] Bob Bossons is up there hollering for us to show 'em the picture.

"So we decide to show 'em the picture. We get all fired up in the huddle, charge up to the ball, hike it, and we get killed. Then someone will holler out first and ten and one of the guys will look at me and say, 'Let's quick kick', or 'How about a long, incomplete pass'."

On days when Jake or Rocky Elton breaks away for long runs or Len Stream connects with an end for a bomb, Jake can be heard to taunt the first stringers with "The price of hamburger just went up."

Do the bombers have a philosophy? "You bet," says Jake. "You gotta have a sense of humor to play with this team. But we take our work seriously. We figure that if we get beat out there on Saturday it's either because our opponent was just too good, or we didn't do our job during the week."

About the sense of humor, Jake says, "We plan to pick up an All-Pro Burger team at the end of the year, and I plan to be on it."

"That's not too surprising," says Salem, "considering there are only about eleven men on the team and Jake'll probably do the choosing himself."

Return of the Autumn Warrior

My introduction to Murray Warmath, the longtime coach for the University of Minnesota Gophers football team, was a rocky one.

While a student at the university, I was a sportswriter for the *Minnesota Daily*, and as such I was a fairly frequent visitor to Warmath's practices. One day I was surprised to see the Gophers running from an unbalanced line with Bobby Bell lining up at tackle as an eligible receiver. Time and again he'd slip off the end of the line to take a short pass from quarterback Sandy Stephens. I thought my readers would enjoy knowing about it.

The next day, I was in the sports information office looking for a photo when one of Warmath's assistants came calling.

"You Mona?" he asked.

I told him I was, and he said, "Coach wants to see you." There were about eight assistant coaches, but only one that all the coaches referred to as "Coach." It was clear I had an appointment with Coach Warmath, with whom I'd never had a one-on-one meeting.

As I entered his Cooke Hall office, he looked up from his desk, where the *Daily* was opened to the page with my article.

"Interesting story here in today's paper," he offered. Somehow it didn't feel like a compliment.

He gestured to a stack of student newspapers from all of the other Big Ten schools. "You can find some real interesting things in these here papers."

His point was clear.

"Son, we're happy to have you fellows at our practices. But sometimes you're going to see some things we'd just as soon not read about the next day. If you have any questions about that kind of thing, I'd appreciate it if you just ask me or one of my assistants. Any questions?"

I couldn't think of any.

Warmath retired as the football coach after the 1971 season, ending an eighteen-year tenure in which his Gophers twice tied for the Big Ten title and earned two trips to the Rose Bowl (1960 and 1961).

It is well documented that the University of Minnesota hasn't won or tied for a Big Ten football championship since 1967. No one knows that date better than the proud members of that squad, many of whom still live in or near the Twin Cities.

When an invitation went out for a reunion several years ago, it was no surprise that the response was outstanding. Mac Boston, Ezell Jones, Chip Litton, Charlie Sanders, Jim Carter, Ron King, John Williams, Walt Bowser, Bob Stein, Del Jessen, Dick Enderle, and three dozen more were quick to respond. I was pleased to be able to emcee the event, especially after the bad start I'd had with Coach Warmath.

It was clear that guys from that 1967 team still enjoyed one another's company. There was a short program. A number of players spoke, but the chance to wind up the evening fell to the team's coach, Murray Warmath, now in his nineties and confined to a wheelchair.

As the coach took the microphone, a silence fell over the crowd. No one knew what to expect from the man they both feared and loved.

Murray was silent for a minute, just looking at the players one by one. Then slowly and somewhat softly he began to speak.

"I know how hard I was on you boys," he said. "I know you were dog tired and we made you run one more drill. I know we probably got in your face and yelled at you maybe a little too often. I know we pushed you beyond what we had any right to expect. But, after all these years, you need to know that when we hollered at you, when we pushed you and when we ran you until you were exhausted— well, it hurt me just as much as it hurt you."

Grown men wiped tears from their eyes as Murray waited, his head slightly bowed.

Then he raised his head, grinned, and said in his familiar southern voice, "NO IT DIDN'T."

It was suddenly forty years earlier, and Warmath was back in charge. He told one player he needed to lose forty pounds. He asked others what happened to their hair. Anyone with facial hair was a sure target.

For the next fifteen minutes, the head coach had their attention, and it was as good as any halftime speech he ever delivered.

Would You Like Me to Write a Sports Story?

To say I knew Garrison Keillor well would be a gross exaggeration—despite the fact that our offices as students at the University of Minnesota were adjacent to each other in the basement of Murphy Hall.

I was a sports reporter and, eventually, the sports editor of the *Minnesota Daily*. Keillor was the leading contributor and editor of *The Ivory Tower*, the campus literary magazine. He wrote well-crafted prose and poetry, whereas I calculated earned run averages. We existed in two different worlds, separated by about three feet.

I think I knew who he was for more than two years before I ever said anything beyond the obligatory "hi" or its longer form, "how's it going?"

One day midway through my senior year, a new edition of *The Ivory Tower* was released, and I heard about it from friends even before I made my usual morning visit to the *Daily* offices.

Keillor and his literary henchmen had been collecting headlines and lead paragraphs from the *Daily* sports section for months. His article reprinted them and then reinterpreted them into English. Had I not written more than a fair share of them, I would have laughed out loud. I may have mentioned that to a few people around the *Daily* office.

The next day Keillor appeared at my door.

"I understand you're upset," he said. "I was rather hoping you'd be amused."

This was more than the combined words we had exchanged in the last two years.

I said he clearly didn't understand what we were trying to say, and that if he were a sports fan, he would not have needed the translation. He looked hurt.

"But I am a sports fan," he protested.

I knew I had him.

"Well, you'd never know it from reading anything you've written."

"Would you like me to write a sports story?" he asked.

I told him that was an excellent idea, never thinking he would take me up on it. I assumed he would wander back to the shores of Lake Wobegon, and I would never hear from him again.

I could not have been more wrong.

Keillor called Gopher hockey star Doug Woog to say he'd like to hang around with him for a while to get some background for a hockey story.

"You can imagine how surprised I was when this guy showed up at my door," Woog later told me. "He wasn't like any sportswriter I ever met. He spoke an entire different language. I'm pretty sure he was the smartest guy I ever met up to that time."

The subsequent issue of *The Ivory Tower* had what I thought at the time was the best sports story I had ever read.

I don't want to say, "I told you so," but from that moment on, I thought Keillor might have a fairly decent future. I only wish I had gotten to know him better when I had the chance.

Mays of Minneapolis

The grading rules were as simple as they were difficult. In order to get an A in magazine writing, you needed to sell a story and get an agreement by the end of the quarter to have the story published. The students met for an hour three times a week with our professor, George Hage.

Because the quarter was only thirteen weeks long, we were supposed to have our idea by the end of the third week. We then needed to write the story to Hage's satisfaction—no easy task. At the same time, we needed to produce a list of publications that might be interested in paying for the story. We then had to research those publications. Who was the editor? What was their address? Did they accept unsolicited manuscripts?

While polishing our ideas, we began sending out pitch letters and sharing the results with our classmates. Each class began with news of rejections as the tension began to mount.

My idea for an article was an in-depth look at Willie Mays' brief stint as center fielder for the Minneapolis Millers. For nearly two months in 1951, Mays had put together one of the great runs in minor league history before being called up to the parent New York Giants. My research showed there was plenty of material about the future Hall of Famer as a Giant, but relatively little, and nothing recent, about Mays' stay in Minneapolis.

Professor Hage said he thought the story had merit and suggested I write several opening paragraphs to submit with my inquiry. I was convinced that I was about to witness a bidding war between *Sport* and *Sports Illustrated*.

The rejection notes arrived the same week, and I shared them with my classmates.

Most of us were reaching for the top of the consumer publications ladder, except for one coed with a rural background who received the green light to submit her piece on bovine research to a breeding publication. They would pay twenty-five dollars, and they wanted the piece immediately.

Professor Hage smiled as we lowered our expectations.

I began to look locally as the end-of-quarter fear began to take hold. With a week remaining in the quarter, I got a phone call. The *Twin Citian* magazine wanted to run the Mays story.

Nothing we had learned in class prepared me for the next question.

"How much would you need to produce that story for us?" the caller asked.

The only thing I could think of was that Willie Mays should bring more than bovine research.

"I think I could do it for thirty dollars," I said.

He said that was within their budget. Years later he told me he would have gone all the way to fifty dollars, but the important thing was to get the promise of publication.

"Will there be anything else?" he asked, after we had agreed on a submission date.

"This may sound a little ungrateful," I said, "but is there any way you could put in writing what we just agreed to?"

"Oh my God," he said. "Are you in Hage's magazine class? I was there about ten years ago. Happy to help you out with an A."

Days of Mays

Following is a reprint of the Willie Mays story that appeared in the Twin Citian *magazine and is discussed in the preceding section. The article appeared with the headline: "Days of Mays: He breezed through town in one spectacular month, just long enough to create a legend."*

The floppy-haired nine-year-old ripped the paper away, stuffed the pink slab of gum into his already full mouth and filed the card into a group held together by a thick rubber band and marked "San Francisco Giants."

"Who'd you get?" asked the boy's father, a 41-year-old Minneapolis businessman.

"Willie Mays," answered the boy. "It says on the back that he played in Minneapolis. Do you remember him?"

Does it rain in a rain forest? Of course he remembers Willie. Not as the veteran of twelve seasons of major league baseball, but as the 19-year-old rookie center fielder who recorded one of the most spectacular months in the history of baseball and won the hearts of a city of traditionally apathetic baseball fans.

The Minneapolis Millers, a charter member of the now defunct American Association, traditionally opened their season on the road to avoid the cold early spring temperatures. On May 1, 1951, the Millers came to Minneapolis after the opening road swing through the esastern cities of the Association.

Halsey Hall, then a columnist for *The Minneapolis Tribune* and now the color man on the Minnesota Twins broadcasts, wrote that day, "Worry about Willie Mays has just about evaporated. He has made the swing through the East now, has faced all kinds of pitching, and has been held hitless in only one game. His throwing power has lived up to reputation, occasionally off target, but powerful. We think you'll like Willie."

Hall was wrong. Minneapolis did not like Willie. They loved and adopted him. Old fans of seventy loved him because he did things they had never seen before. He hit doubles to the opposite field on pitches intended for intentional walks. He led off base three feet outside the accepted limits, and would score from first on a single.

Kids loved Willie because he came early to games and stayed late to sign autographs. He kept broken bats to give to the little leaguers who waited faithfully outside the gate after each game.

General Manager Rosy Ryan loved Mays because he packed fans into ancient Nicollet Park in hopes of seeing one of the famous basket catches or belly-first slides into second on a stolen base.

Teammates loved Willie because of his cheerful "Say-hey," which would go far to brighten any situation.

On May 2, 6,477 shivering fans, including Mayor Eric Hoyer and Governor Luther Youngdahl, crowded into the wooden park to watch the Millers drub Columbus 11 to 0. Mays collected three hits in five attempts, including one home run.

Four stories deserved special attention on the local sports page the next day. The Millers rated top billing. Second space went to a young shortstop from Minneapolis Central high school named Johnny Blanchard who raised his batting average to .750 and was supposedly talking to New York Yankee scouts about signing a contract after graduation. A young freshman quarterback named Paul Giel was drawing raves from his University of Minnesota Coach, Wes Fesler. Buried in an obscure corner was the news that the parent New York Giants had lost their eleventh consecutive game and were seeking outfield help.

Day after day Mays continued his torrid hitting, and his batting average slowly climbed over the .400 mark. The Millers were gaining on the first place Milwaukee Brewers, and the Giants were mired in seventh place in the eight-team National League.

Local sportswriters began to write apprehensive columns telling why the Giants shouldn't do the inevitable and call up Mays.

Joe Hendrickson, another *Tribune* columnist, said, "Don't Do It, Leo! The Giants should have learned a lesson last year in the Tookie Gilbert case. After temporarily ruining him by throwing him in the big fire too soon, it is unlikely the Giants' front office will singe Mays. Rosy Ryan thinks two years of Triple A ball would make the spectacular Mays a cinch star in the big show.

"Furthermore, right field is the problem spot for the Giants at this time. The short, tricky right field fence in the Polo Grounds would not give Mays a fair chance to show his skill."

But Hendrickson and others didn't foresee that the Giants thought enough of Mays to move Bobby Thomson to left, Whitey Lockman to first, Monte Irvin to right, and drop Don Mueller from the starting lineup to make room for Mays.

Willie Mays of the Minneapolis Millers, 1951.
Photo by Minneapolis Star Tribune, *from the Minnesota Historical Society*

On May 11, Giant scout Hank DeBerry watched Mays go three for four to raise his average to .453. Before reporting back to Giant Manager Leo Durocher and General Manager Horace Stoneham in New York, DeBerry told reporters, "Don't worry about Willie Mays. He belongs right here."

The next day Willie had three teeth pulled and played only briefly in the next three games. On May 14, Mays returned to the starting lineup. Hall, in his game story, said, "In the second game of the doubleheader Windy McCall of the Indianapolis Indians got Mays out twice in a row. Heath [the Millers manager] was going to bench him. It was the second time in a WEEK that any pitcher had done this. Well, a slump's a slump. Anyway, he's hitting .482."

On May 19, the weather got warmer and Mays kept pace. He went four for five and raised his average to .493. During the third week in May the Giants tried four right fielders in six games and didn't produce a single hit.

The night of the 24th found the Millers in Kansas City. They were one game out of first place and two days away from the crucial series with league-leading Milwaukee. The Giants were in fifth, 4½ games out of first.

Minneapolis had played an afternoon game and Willie went to a Western movie in downtown Kansas City. He recalls, "I was sitting in the movie and the manager of the theater came out on the stage and said for me to get in touch with Tommy Heath at the hotel.

"When I got to the hotel Heath told me I was going up to the Giants. 'Who said so?' I asked Heath. 'Leo Durocher,' he said. 'Not me.' I said, 'call him up and tell him I'm not coming.'

"Heath looked at me like I was crazy or something, then called New York. When he got Durocher, he put me on the phone. Durocher was mad. 'What do you mean, you're not coming up?' he yelled. 'I can't play in the big leagues,' I told him.

"'Why can't you?' he asked. 'I can't hit enough up there,' I told him. 'What are you hitting now?' he asked.

"'.477,' I told him.

"There was a silence on the phone. I'm not sure but I thought I heard someone laugh at the other end of the line. Finally I heard him bark: 'Hurry up and get your tail up here before I come down for you myself.'"

So Willie left Minneapolis: The headlines demanded blood.

Hall said, "In many respects it was a vile trick." The only saving grace of the situation was its inevitability.

The evening paper that day compared Mays to Ted Williams, another superstar who was recalled from Minneapolis by the Boston Red Sox in 1938.

That night's top sport story wasn't a story at all. It was a poem labeled, "But There Is No Joy at Nicollet," written by the entire sports staff in the style of the most famous of all baseball poems, "Casey At The Bat." It ended with these lines:

"Oh, somewhere in this favored land the sun is shining bright.

And somewhere bands are playing, and somewhere hearts
are light.

And somewhere kids are singing, and feeling gay and silly.

But there is no joy at Nicollet: the Giants called up Willie."

During the first week of Willie's absence Miller fans knocked everyone from Stoneham to the Giant bat boy. Hendrickson crucified Durocher in installment form. Hundreds of readers wrote to suggest fitting punishment for Durocher and Stoneham.

Finally Stoneham bought space in the Minneapolis papers and ran an apology for taking Willie and listed reasons in his defense.

When Willie left Minneapolis he had 71 hits in 149 at-bats, was hitting .477, had eight home runs, and 31 runs batted in, and had made but one error in 95 chances.

He started slowly with the Giants and asked Durocher to be sent back to Minneapolis. The Giant manager would have nothing to do with such nonsense. He stuck by Mays and was rewarded when Willie finished the season hitting .274 and was named Rookie of The Year.

Just for the record the Giants won the pennant that year because of Mays and a home run by Bobby Thomson in the ninth inning of the final playoff game against the Brooklyn Dodgers. The Millers finished in fifth place, 17½ games out of first.

The *Bedtime Nooz*

I wasn't really surprised when the Minneapolis Public Schools did not renew any of us for our summer jobs. I knew I wasn't going to miss unloading those boxcars.

But I still needed a summer job, and it was already early May. At eighteen, I figured I was far too sophisticated to return to my previous jobs as a bagger at Red Owl and a catalog order filler at Sears.

It was my mother who reminded me that WCCO TV had given me a four-year scholarship to the University of Minnesota and suggested that they might have something in the way of summer employment.

Harboring low expectations, I called Tom Cousins, the station's promotions director, to ask if they had any summer openings.

"There's a fair amount of turnover in the newsroom," he said. "Come on down and I'll set up an interview with the news director, Joe Bartelme."

So, after morning classes as a freshman journalism student at the University of Minnesota, I crossed the river into downtown Minneapolis to explore career possibilities in journalism.

"Can you spell?" Bartelme asked.

"How many hours a week could you work?"

"Can you start tomorrow?"

I must really be making a good first impression, I thought.

Turns out someone had quit a few hours before I got there and gave two days' notice. Timing is everything.

I began working twenty hours a week as a dispatcher in the Channel 4 newsroom. It was the perfect job for a journalism student. Need to do an editorial for class? Get some advice from George Rice, one of the few broadcasters in the nation to do a daily editorial as part of the ten o'clock news. Want to do a piece on state government? How about an introduction from chief legislative reporter and future CBS White House correspondent Phil Jones?

By far the best part of working at WCCO TV was working with Dave Moore. His ego was as small as his talent was large. Anyone who worked long with Dave had a chance to see how he handled the many admirers he encountered every time he made his way through downtown Minneapolis.

"Oh, Mr. Moore," a fan would say, "I really admire the way you do the news."

Almost without fail, Dave would sigh and say, "You know what I really do? I read words that people write for me. If you want to admire someone, admire a person who really does something. Admire a cop or that person who's teaching your sons and daughters."

Dave was an actor at heart. Good as he was at reading the news, acting was his passion. He was a student when Tim Ramsland, a distant cousin of mine, was the head of the drama department at the University of Minnesota.

"He was the best young actor I ever saw," Ramsland once told me. "Absolutely the best."

Many years after I left WCCO TV, I was a member of a group called The Spectators. We met every other Friday afternoon with guests from the world of sports. Dave Moore was just a member. No more, no less. When the basket came around, he put his five dollars in the same way everyone else did.

One year it was my turn to chair the group. The main duties of the chair centered around getting the guest speakers and running the meetings. It wasn't exactly heavy lifting, but the hardest part by far was getting more than twenty uncompensated speakers to give up a spare noon hour.

The average Spectator was male and in his early fifties. Many of them were working for the first person or firm to offer them a job after the end of World War II.

One of my guests was one in a series of new sportscasters on KSTP TV. He did not share Dave Moore's lack of ego. Our guest got through his remarks well enough and was ready for some questions.

"How did your career take you to KSTP?" a member asked.

There it was. A perfect seventy-five-mile-an-hour fastball down the heart of the plate.

"Well," he said, "I was working in Oklahoma City, which was the forty-seventh-largest market in the country. When I started, we were number three in the market, but within two years we were number one. I sent some tapes out and it wasn't long before I got an offer in Omaha. That was the thirty-fifth-largest market, so I said so long to

Oklahoma City and hello to Omaha. It was pretty much the same story there. Started out as the number three station in the market, but within a couple of years we had the top-rated sports show in town. So we sent out the tapes and pretty soon I got an offer from Denver, which was the sixteenth-largest market. I accepted that job, but before I started I got a call from KSTP. This was the thirteenth-largest market, so I told Denver no way, and that's how I got to the Twin Cities."

The Spectators were unimpressed. Many were appalled at the obvious lack of loyalty. My guest, smart enough to know he was bombing with his audience, looked for a lifeline and spotted Dave Moore.

Relieved, he said, "I'm sure it's similar to the way Mr. Moore there got his start."

All eyes turned to Dave.

He slowly shook his head and said, "Oh, hell no. I just stopped in there to use the can one day and they asked me to read something. I've been on the air ever since."

In the early 1960s Dave wanted to do a different kind of news, a kind that would allow him to use both his sense of humor and his acting skills. This was two decades before *That Was the Week That Was* and *Laugh-In*, and three decades before *Saturday Night Live*.

On Saturday nights, after the 10 p.m. news, Dave and most of the writers and editors headed out the back door of the station, across

LaSalle Avenue, down the alley, and into Duff's, arguably the best bar in the Twin Cities in terms of interesting clientele.

While they talked and planned at Duff's, the station was running Critic's Award Theater. This was years before cable. The show was sponsored by the Iron Mining Industry of Minnesota. If viewers were willing to sit through a ten-minute infomercial, they would be rewarded with an uncut, full-length movie. The idea was revolutionary and incredibly popular, especially among babysitters.

The creative Moore saw this as an opportunity.

He talked a single camera operator into staying around after the Critic's Award Theater for a new show that Dave was going to write. He called it the *Bedtime Nooz*, and he never did tell the management about it. As far as they knew, their uninterrupted movie was followed by the national anthem and signoff.

But Moore's show was gathering a cult following. Babysitters begged parents to let them stay a few minutes more so they could see the *Bedtime Nooz*. People coming home from bars were finding a new breed of news.

And they liked it.

One day the inevitable happened. An advertising executive, most likely one with young children, called the station to find out how much it would cost to sponsor the *Bedtime Nooz*.

Station executives thought Moore would be thrilled, but his

reaction was just the opposite. With sponsorship came responsibility. The *Bedtime Nooz* was about irresponsibility.

What's worse, the station had sold the sponsor two one-minute spots plus an opening and closing billboard. That was another problem. Some nights the *Bedtime Nooz* wasn't more than three minutes long. It was as long as Dave wrote it, and now it was supposed to contain two one-minute spots. Dave didn't like executives messing with his creation.

Bartelme, the news director, promised help. His eyes searched the newsroom for someone who would give up every Saturday night for the paltry budget he had at his disposal.

"Mona," he yelled. "I need to see you. Now!"

Joe didn't exactly have a private office, but his desk was set away from the reporters and editors. He usually spoke in a loud voice, but he always lowered his voice when the subject was money.

"This could be your big chance in journalism," he told this college sophomore, "and we don't expect you to do this for the same money you make as a dispatcher. So, for the hours you work on the *Bedtime Nooz* we'll pay you a dollar-seventy-five an hour rather than a dollar-fifty an hour."

I was overwhelmed. Think of all the things I could do with that extra dollar-fifty. Buy a house? A car? A cheeseburger?

I accepted on the spot. As I got up to leave, Bartelme lowered his voice and said, "About that extra money—I'd appreciate it if you didn't mention it to the other guys."

"Don't worry," I managed to reassure him. "I'm as embarrassed about it as you are."

I worked closely with Dave Moore for the next two years. He could read copy like nobody I would ever work with again. He could do voices. He could deliver punch lines, and he could make a writer feel as if it were the copy and not the actor that was responsible for the success of the program.

It's too bad that the station did not get its first videotape machine until late 1964. Very few of the early *Bedtime Nooz* episodes were preserved.

As a footnote, those commercials that set Dave off against management turned out to be some of his best work. They were for the Sealy mattress company. Dave wrote them and starred in them. Several decades later, a very successful Twin Cities advertising executive said he thought Dave's Sealy ads were among the best he had ever seen.

Dave would have gently disagreed.

Election Night

Heading into the fall of 1964, the ratings race between the ten o'clock news on WCCO TV, anchored by Dave Moore, and the KSTP TV offering, anchored by John MacDougall, was about dead even.

The brain wizards upstairs had something big in mind, but word of the exact plan was slow in making its way to the belowground newsroom.

In late October, the station dropped a promotional bombshell on the Twin Cities television market. Interest in the upcoming presidential election was enormous, with local favorite Hubert Humphrey paired as Lyndon Johnson's running mate against Arizona Republican Barry Goldwater and his long-forgotten running mate, William Miller.

Predictions of record turnouts filled the pages of *The Minneapolis Star* and *The Minneapolis Tribune*. There were no statewide elections because the state had gone to four-year terms two years earlier when Karl Rolvaag had defeated Elmer Anderson by just ninety-one votes.

With what was supposed to be a very close presidential election dominating the evening news every night, WCCO made a dramatic move. In two weeks it would be joining forces with emerging computer giant Control Data to provide the first computerized election returns.

It was a brilliant move. Although it would be two decades before computers made an impact in our homes, they evoked a mixture of awe and respect among the general public.

Virtually every promotion piece in the two-week period touted the high-speed partnership. If Hubert Humphrey was going to be the next vice president of the United States, you would learn about it courtesy of Dave Moore and Control Data.

Studio Four, the site of the ten-o'clock newscast each night, was converted to "Election Central," with banks of computers and low-tech tote boards ready to post the early results. The tote boards consisted of plywood slat wall with a series of hooks from which hung the names of the candidates. To their left was a series of seven spinning numbers, each with ten facings from one to ten.

As a full-time college student and part-time employee, my job that night was the lowliest in the place. I was the number spinner, and my only assignment was to keep moving fast enough to avoid the sweep of the camera as it moved from the presidential election to the results of voting on the Taconite Amendment. (The Taconite Amendment sought to lower the taxes that were levied on mining companies, and thus help to revitalize the mining industry in northern Minnesota. The amendment won approval from the voters.)

My part wasn't particularly glamorous, but even the jaded reporters realized that the marriage of computers and election returns was clearly at the leading edge of an unstoppable wave. The excitement was palpable in the newsroom and the studio as the night advanced. Reporters wore their nicest suits and best ties (they were all men at the time). I proudly donned the blue blazer that had served me so well at high school graduation more than three years earlier. I complemented it with a nifty blue Gant shirt purchased at Dayton's Northbriar shop earlier in the day.

The polls closed at 8 p.m. At exactly 7:59:50, a call for silence swept the studio.

Eleven seconds later Dave Moore, in a calm but excited voice, told viewers they were in for a special treat, as the first computerized election returns were just minutes away. About a dozen computer operators, all in short-sleeved white shirts and thin neckties, eagerly stood by their gigantic machines. Phil Jones, standing by at Humphrey headquarters, told viewers that all eyes there were on the WCCO computerized election returns. It was the same story with Bob Fahs at Republican headquarters.

Moore was back thirty minutes later to tell viewers that he would be back at nine with the early returns. At least that was the plan.

Nobody got nervous until about 8:45.

"Shouldn't we be getting something out of these machines?" asked news director Joe Bartelme, who was nervous under almost any circumstances. He lit one cigarette off the end of another and paced. A jittery Bartelme could have undone Cool Hand Luke.

At 8:50 even the usually cool Moore was visibly nervous as he paced between the computers and his anchor slot, rolling and unrolling his opening script. The computer operators offered little consolation. They processed numbers, they reminded us. They didn't create them.

"We better be getting some numbers pretty goddamn soon," Bartelme said, "or we'll all be looking for work." That certainly helped lower the tension.

At 8:59 the studio was in full meltdown mode. We would be on the air in sixty seconds, and we didn't have one return. About two-thirds of the TV sets in the region would be tuning in.

Bartelme needed to come up with something fast.

"Mona," he screamed, "get me some early returns and get them up fast. And don't give me anything that's gonna embarrass us later."

Sensing a rare opportunity to not only influence history but to create it, I dashed to the boards. It was clear that Moore would lead with the presidential returns, so that's where I started.

"Good evening," Moore said to the viewers as I reached for the Johnson/Humphrey numbers. My mind was moving as fast as my hands. The first votes were most likely to come in from the Twin Cities, where Humphrey's popularity should make a difference.

"Taking a look at the presidential race, where we have the very earliest of our computerized returns for the evening . . . ."

I slid quickly to my right as the cameras showed:

6,778   Johnson/Humphrey

4,911   Goldwater/Miller

"Keep in mind," Moore said, "the polls have been closed only an hour and these are most likely the first returns from the Twin Cities area."

Listening to Moore, I tried to judge how much time I had to create my returns.

"Looking at what is expected to be a tight race for the U.S. Senate seat . . . ," he continued.

Seconds earlier, sensing a good night for DFLers, I had posted the following:

5,507   Eugene McCarthy

5,222   Wheelock Whitney

Moving with the speed of Moore, I rapidly created small leads for all the favorites in the races for the House of Representatives: Don Fraser over Walter Judd by fewer than a hundred votes; Clark McGregor by a wide margin over Richard Parish in the Republican-safe Third District; and incumbent Joseph Karth up on challenger John Drexler in the Fourth District.

The Taconite Amendment, thought to be very popular with voters, was well on its way to victory.

Moore touched on each board no more than five seconds after my creation.

We cut away to Jones, who showed crowds of cheering Democrats at a local hotel. My numbers were much more popular with Jones' audience than they were with Fahs' at Republican headquarters.

While Fahs was interviewing a Republican strategist, the wire service machines roared to life in a corner of the studio.

Johnson/Humphrey: 6,778

Goldwater/Miller: 4,911

Every one of our results had been flashed to every Associated Press and United Press International outlet in the region. There was no question they had bought into our promotions.

Those of us who were in on the sleight of hand toasted our approval at the wire report, but the celebration lasted less than a minute as the computers began spitting out numbers that rapidly made our initial reports of little memory or importance.

Updating the election results on WCCO TV, 1964

We worked through the night. The computerized election results were an unqualified success in their speed and accuracy and, ultimately, in the ratings numbers that showed up later that fall.

By midnight I knew that every one of my early leaders had won. The vote totals were hundreds of times larger than my opening numbers, and people neither remembered nor cared about those very first returns.

I don't recall that anyone inside the studio made much of our numbers game as the excitement and activity of the evening rolled on. The ratings were huge, and election coverage locally and across the nation was never the same.

My Friend the Serial Killer

I was early for a meeting of the University of Minnesota Journalism School's alumni and had time to look for some interesting conversation. Right behind me was Ron Handberg. Ron and I had worked together in the WCCO TV newsroom in the 1960s, some forty years earlier. He went on to become the station's news director and general manager. He also wrote several locally based murder mysteries.

Because he spent parts of four decades at WCCO, he is a great source of information about the eventual landing spots for WCCO alumni. I started with the easy ones. Whatever happened to Skip Loescher? How about Quent Neufeld? Susan Spencer? Barry Peterson? Bob McNamara?

Gradually I moved the discussion back to the reporters who were there during the three years I worked there. These were the young guys who broke into television news as it was exploding nationwide.

Is it true that Jim Kirk died early? What happened to Pete Hively? Bob Fahs? Sam Taylor? Phil Jones?

Handberg had an answer for every one of my questions.

Bob Spangler?

Something changed in his demeanor. "You knew Bob Spangler?"

I didn't know him that well. He left the station several months after I started as a dispatcher in the newsroom, and his departure may have been the reason that Handberg migrated from the WCCO Radio newsroom to WCCO TV.

"You know about Spangler," he said.

"I don't know anything about him except that he came to WCCO from Iowa like a lot of guys in the newsroom. I think I was the one who met a delivery person at the front desk and carried Bob's going-away cake down to the newsroom. Aside from that, I can barely remember him. Why? Is there something I missed?"

Handberg said we needed to talk, and we moved to an out-of-the way spot at the McNamara Alumni Center, where he filled me in on the details flowing out of my seemingly innocuous question.

"Bob Spangler turned out to be one of the bigger serial killers in the history of the country," he said.

He had my full attention.

Turns out Bob was born in Des Moines and adopted at an early age by Merlin and Ione Spangler. His father became a well-known and respected member of the Iowa State faculty. He co-developed a widely used theory on the effect of soil pressure on underground conduits. There is a building named for him on the Iowa State University campus.

Bob graduated from Iowa State with a degree in technical journalism. He got married and moved to Minnesota. His son, David, was born in 1961, and his daughter, Susan, was born in 1963, about the time Bob left WCCO for a job in Colorado.

Fifteen years later in Littleton, Colorado, the killing began.

Susan's boyfriend, failing to get an answer to phone calls or knocks on the door of the Spangler home, entered the home through a basement window and found his girlfriend shot dead in her bed. Her brother had been shot and killed in an adjacent room. A search of the house turned up a third body, Bob's wife, Nancy Spangler. She had died from a single shot. The gun was found near her, along with a typewritten suicide note signed with the initial "N."

Bob returned home from the movie theater to find police cars and the coroner at his house. There were a number of suspicions, but no hard evidence connecting Spangler to the killings. A handwriting analyst confirmed it was his wife's handwriting on the initialed letter.

Seven months later, to the shock and disbelief of his friends, he married a woman with whom he had been having a long-term affair. She was an avid hiker who loved to visit the Grand Canyon. In 1986 she published a book, *One Foot in the Grand Canyon*, which was a modest success among fellow hikers.

That same year, Bob, feeling some financial pressures, went to visit his ninety-two-year-old father, who was still in good health. According to later reports, Bob asked his father for money. A few days after Bob's arrival, his father took a serious fall down a flight of stairs. He died within two weeks, leaving Bob enough money to retire comfortably.

Within a year, second wife Sharon, suffering from depression and claiming to be afraid of her husband, sued for divorce. The settlement meant Bob had to go back to work as a radio talk show host, but he was able to insert a clause into the decree that said some $20,000 of the settlement would revert to him if she died before he did.

Lonely, Spangler turned to the personal columns for friendship and quickly hooked up with Donna Sundling, a personal fitness instructor. They were married in 1990.

The marriage had problems from the start, and there was talk of a separation. Bob suggested that a hiking trip to the Grand Canyon might help solve things. They camped overnight near one of the most dangerous trails in his second wife's book. The next day, while taking a photo from a precarious angle, Donna fell to her death, according to the story Spangler told local authorities.

Once again, there were suspicions of foul play, but no hard evidence against Spangler. Donna's adult children, knowing their mother's extreme fear of heights, pressed authorities to look more closely at Spangler as a suspect.

Shortly after the death of his third wife, Spangler's second wife moved back in with him, but her depression persisted. Five months later she took an overdose of prescription drugs and was hospitalized. Although doctors did not think the dose was enough to be fatal, she died in the hospital with her ex-husband at her side.

Bob now had three dead wives, two dead children, and a dead father, all of whom had died under suspicious circumstances. Police and the FBI started building an extensive file on him.

Meanwhile, in August 2000, Bob started having serious medical problems. He was diagnosed with inoperable lung cancer at age sixty-seven.

Law enforcement authorities brought him in for questioning. Playing to his huge ego, they paraded him past boxes clearly marked "Spangler Murder Investigation."

Aware that he was dying, he seemed eager to talk. The authorities mentioned that the case had been reviewed by a "serial murder profiler." Spangler seemed fascinated by the profiler and wanted to talk to him. Police said the profiler worked only on serial killers.

"How many does it take to be a serial killer?" he asked.

"Three or more," they replied.

Spangler asked for the chance to make a phone call to his fourth wife.

A few minutes later he told authorities, "You've got your serial killer."

He subsequently confessed to the killing of his first wife and children and to the murder of his third wife at the Grand Canyon. He was quoted as telling authorities that with the exception of those two days, he lived a good, law-abiding life.

He admitted to typing his first wife's suicide note and sliding it in among some papers he asked her to initial. He said he shot his daughter first and then shot his son, who didn't die right away. He then suffocated his son with his pillow. Lastly, he shot and killed his wife. He placed the suicide note beside her and put a chair next to the closet shelf where he kept his gun.

He said he killed his third wife by luring her to one of the most dangerous parts of the Grand Canyon. At that point, knowing that the 160-foot fall would be fatal, he shoved her over the edge. He then climbed down to survey his work, covered her body with a tarp, and went in search of authorities.

His background as a television journalist and radio personality, combined with an outgoing personality, made him a convincing storyteller.

His medical condition worsening, he never went through a trial. He died the next year in the Federal Corrections Medical Facility in Springfield, Missouri, some ten months after being taken into custody and twenty-three years after killing his first wife and children.

Spangler's exploits are the subject of at least two books, and he has been featured on several cable television documentaries. His personal story turns out to be a lot more memorable than anything he did in his short career at WCCO TV.

100 Years from Now

I never would have identified Jim Hopkins among my greatest teachers, but I learned as much from that man as anyone I've ever known.

Hoppy, who was sixty-three when I met him as a twenty-one-year-old, was the editor of the late shift at *The Minneapolis Tribune*. Legend had it that in his earlier years, the Oklahoma native had told

A fresh-faced young reporter at *The Minneapolis Tribune*

a young Walter Cronkite that he might have a future in journalism if he worked harder at learning how to write.

By the time I met Hoppy, he had no illusions about promotion. All he wanted to do was put out a decent newspaper each morning with as little hassle as possible. He didn't tell jokes, but he had a way of saying things, honed over five decades in various newsrooms, that connected with young reporters. Casual profanity was part of nearly every sentence. It was part of what endeared him to his staff.

As the first deadline approached, Hoppy was more predictable and more effective than any mechanical device.

"Parsons," he would shout across the newsroom at Jim Parsons, the slowest writer in the newsroom who also understood that there was a series of deadlines and the only one that really mattered was the last one.

"Parsons, you gonna be turning that masterpiece in any time soon?"

"Parsons, there's five minutes 'til deadline and you're just sitting there looking at your typewriter. The goddamn thing don't work until you start hitting some of those keys."

"Parsons, I got nine other people here waiting to go over to the Little Wagon, and you've got just three minutes to turn that story in."

"All right, goddamn it, Parsons, just gimme what you got written. Goddamn it, one hundred years from now, ain't nobody gonna know the difference."

We started to call them Hoppyisms, and when he retired we did a version of the newspaper filled with them.

Like many career newspapermen, Hoppy disliked management. Openly.

"The funny thing about [managing editor Daryl] Feldmeier, he used to be a damn fine reporter," Hoppy would muse in a voice just loud enough to be heard in the nearby executive offices.

One day, a recent Northwestern University honors graduate turned in a traffic story that caught Hoppy's attention. Copy in hand, he shuffled to her desk.

"Read me that lead paragraph," he said.

Not sensing what was coming, she read, "An elderly Minneapolis woman was killed while crossing Hiawatha Avenue Tuesday morning."

"Goddamn it, Susan," he said, "the woman was sixty-four years old. Since when is a sixty-four-year-old woman elderly? Some day you'll learn to appreciate that. Now rewrite this thing and give it back to me. Fast."

It may not have been in the Associated Press stylebook, but it was another lesson well learned.

Hoppy also hated long stories.

"Lots of little stories that start and end on page one. That's what people want to read."

Often he was charged with deciding what stories would be featured on the front page of the next day's newspaper. When he fretted, he did it aloud.

"I got two stories here longer than a whore's dream and not a hole to put 'em in. Goddamn it, I hate long stories. Nobody reads long stories."

He was equally unforgiving of errors in grammar or punctuation, and he had a set of rules that had never appeared in any of my textbooks. "Goddamn it," he would shout to a new reporter, "commas, like tits, come in pairs. Didn't you learn anything worthwhile in college?"

Hoppy liked Brian Anderson, who for the past twenty-five years has been the editor of *Mpls/St. Paul Magazine*.

"That little sumbitch can write stories that make people smile," Hoppy said. "We don't have enough writers like that, and when we do, nobody appreciates 'em."

Hoppy had never before seen anybody like the young Molly Ivins, who went on to become one of the most insightful political columnists in the country. Molly joined the paper not long before Hoppy collected his pension.

"That's one of the sassiest people I ever met," he said of young Ivins. "She's always workin' her personal opinion into stories, but lawdy, lawdy, I'd hate to get on the wrong side of that woman."

Just ask George W. Bush.

Hoppy moved to Norfolk, Nebraska, after he retired. I visited him there two years after his retirement. When I arrived, he had a copy of the bogus *Tribune* we had done with all his stories and observations.

"This here thing was pretty funny," he said. "Brought back a lot of good memories, but I didn't realize I swore so goddamn much."

Molly Ivins Teaches Us New Words

She was totally unlike any new hire in recent memory. Usually when *The Minneapolis Tribune* hired someone from "outside the market," it was a good bet they were talking about Fargo, Des Moines, or Madison.

Molly was from Texas, and you couldn't miss her. She was loud. She didn't sound like anyone else in the newsroom. And she was tall. If she were a basketball player, she would have been a power forward.

Molly taught us all how to swear. She was good at it, and she knew words we'd never heard before. It was difficult for her to complete a sentence without swearing.

Her favorite word was "sumbitch," which we learned could be either good or bad. For instance: "That dumb sumbitch was so stupid he could dive off the dock and not find water." Or, "You had to admire the way that sumbitch could put words together."

For much of her brief tenure with the *Tribune*, she was assigned to the police beat. They clearly didn't know what to make of her, but legend had it that they named a pet pig "Molly" in her honor.

There was little factual support for most of the stories about Molly. She became a bit of an instant legend. Stu Baird, the genial city editor, once claimed that he had gotten a complaint from the police that her language was too salty. They never offered any proof, but there was little reason to doubt it.

After graduating from Smith College, in Massachusetts, getting a master's in journalism from Columbia University, and spending a year in France, Ivins joined the *Tribune* in the fall of the year, arriving from Texas without an overcoat. A few weeks later she entered the newsroom in a floor-length reddish orange maxi coat, which nicely matched her red hair.

As she walked slowly through the newsroom, assistant managing editor Frank Premack shouted, "My, God, it looks like a bad paint job on the Foshay Tower."

Molly's response to one of the most senior members of the newsroom staff was to perform an impossible anatomical feat upon himself.

There were a lot of rumors about Molly. She once claimed to have shoved Lynda Johnson—daughter of former president Lyndon Johnson—into a lake at summer camp.

When Molly left the *Tribune*, she wrote a magazine article entitled "*The Minneapolis Tribune* Is a Stone Wall Drag." It chronicled her three years at the paper and the reasons so many people left. Today, many of us still have copies of that story, and we were saddened in January 2007 to learn of her death at age sixty-two from an aggressive form of breast cancer.

Her columns were carried in more than four hundred newspapers, and her numerous obituaries included many of her better quotes. She loved to attack Texas politicians and once wrote of one, "If his IQ slips any lower, we'll have to water him twice a day."

While covering emerging politicians in Texas, she began to refer to President George W. Bush alternately as "Shrub" or "Dubya." Upon his election as president, she referred to him as President Billy Bob Forehead.

To Ivins, Arnold Schwarzenegger was "a condom filled with walnuts."

Writing about Bill Clinton during the Monica Lewinsky affair, she referred to his character as "weaker than bus station chili."

No one ever said that about Molly.

Baseball Cards: A Hard Sell

Even from the first days after I joined The Minneapolis Tribune, *I thought there might be a good story around one of my earliest hobbies, collecting baseball cards.*

Unfortunately, my editors didn't share my opinion. Several times I suggested a feature on card collecting, and each time I was rejected. Finally, I approached the editor of the Sunday paper. He offered no promises but said he would consider running the story if I could write it.

I recalled from my days at WCCO TV that Dave Moore's kids were heavily involved in baseball cards. In fact, I had once sorted my doubles from the 1950s and given stacks of them to Dave's sons, Pete and Charley.

I called their home and got sufficient information from their mother, Shirley, to convince me there was enough there to turn into a feature. A call to Topps Baseball Cards provided an envelope full of background material. (What took about a month to research in those days would have been found with a five-minute Google search today.)

Armed with the Moore family's story and the Topps material, I wrote the article that follows, under the headline "Baseball Umpire, 11, Hollers 'Play Cards'." I was proud when the story that no editor had wanted received the Twin

Cities Newspaper Guild's Page One Award for best feature story of 1967.

I was pleased to learn recently from Charley Moore that the dice game described in the article that passed from Dave to his sons has now made its way to another generation of Moores.

In the dead of night several years ago, Shirley Moore stole her sons' baseball cards.

That was the time the boys had threatened to play with them all winter. She wouldn't even give them back as a Christmas present.

And that wasn't the first time she had silently pilfered them. There was the time she and her husband, Dave, got up one morning and decided their Edina home was being taken over by small cardboard pictures of Mickey Mantle, Yogi Berra, and Sandy Koufax.

They found them in the bath tub, in all the beds, on the kitchen table, and in the linings of most of the chairs.

"The next time I have to pick up one of these cards," she announced, preparing to deliver her high hard one, "I'm going to pick them all up—every darn card—and you'll never see them again."

The next day Harmon Killebrew, or maybe it was Marv Throneberry, peeked out from under the rug and Mrs. Moore proceeded to strike out the side.

Sons Pete and Charley protested vehemently. They even went to the den to visit the commissioner, but father Dave, after consulting with the umpire, overruled the protest.

The scene in the Moore dugout is typical of most homes around the country.

Baseball cards originated in the 1880s and are now in their third generation.

The biggest source is Topps Chewing Gum, Inc., New York, N.Y., which distributes about 250 million baseball cards each year.

A spokesman for the company, which has been taken to court several times on charges on monopolizing the industry, said that collecting the cards ranks as "the biggest summertime hobby for youngsters between the ages of 7 and 12 in this country."

About 500 cards are included in Topps' annual series and they are issued at regular intervals.

Area grocers are familiar with the lad who comes in to buy a new box of gum in order to obtain the entire series. Usually, about 89 of the desired 90 cards are in the box, and the lad is left with 30 doubles to trade for the missing card.

Because of the large number of cards produced, individual cards are practically worthless. One ex-collector recalled trading Ted Williams, Sal Maglie, Allie Reynolds, and Bob Feller for one Sibbi Sisti.

A favorite story in baseball-card-collecting circles concerns Honus Wagner, the famous Pittsburgh shortstop of the early 1900s. He discovered that a cigarette company had issued a card with his picture on it.

Wagner, a nonsmoker, protested it, and all the cards were removed from the market. As a result there are only six known cards in this series in existence today. One changed hands recently for $250, making it the most valuable baseball card in existence. [Editor's note: A near-mint-condition Honus Wagner card from the series was sold at auction for $2.8 million dollars in September 2007.]

The cards change every year and new photographs are affixed to the front while the players' statistics are updated on the back of the card.

Each spring photographers take two pictures of each player—one with his cap on, the other bareheaded. The second picture is used in case the player is traded before the card is issued.

The Edina boys' group that plays in the basement of Moore's house is fairly typical of groups around the nation.

Pete Moore, 11; Charley Moore, 13; Craig Soderberg, 11; and Scott Barno, 11, play a game with dice and the cards. Each player owns several teams, and a full schedule, ending with a World Series, is played each year.

The boys learned their game from Moore, a WCCO television newscaster.

He recalls how he used to play the dice game in the basement of his south Minneapolis home with some neighborhood friends. Those friends have grown up to be a history professor at a Big Ten university, business executives, a dentist, and a former baseball player.

"But the kids have modified and sophisticated the game far beyond anything we ever did," Moore said. "They added things like the steal and sacrifice fly on certain combinations."

The scores of the games are reasonably accurate, Charley said, but individual performances are left entirely to chance.

For instance, Brooks Robinson is just about the worst hitter in the American League.

Perhaps the most remarkable part of their game has been the hitting of Dean Chance, the Minnesota Twins pitcher who recently set all kinds of records for nonhitting when he went out 77 times between hits.

In Moore's basement Chance is the hitting star. He won one game for himself with back-to-back home runs.

Charley recalled some trouble in their World Series several years back.

With the Tigers leading in the final game of the series, relief pitcher Phil Regan gave up a last-inning, bases-loaded home run to lose the game and the series.

Charley, then the Detroit manager, got so angry he walked out to the mound and tore Regan in half.

The boys take turns being the American and National League president, commissioner of baseball, and chief statistician.

Craig recently moved to Oregon. "It was too bad," said Dave Moore. " He really didn't want to go. He was due to be commissioner next year.

The Moores say the boys have now reached a happy compromise stage. "They still play with the cards, but they play in the Little League program, too."

The time spent in the basement hasn't been completely wasted, Moore pointed out. "The boys learned to read from the cards."

"Once a relative was quizzing Pete about geography. That was back in 1960 when he was 4. She asked where Pittsburgh was and he'd say in Pennsylvania and she'd ask about St. Louis and he'd say Missouri and finally she said, "Where's Cincinnati?'

"And Pete said, 'In first place.'"

Another time, Charley was being quizzed by a school psychologist on a word knowledge drill.

"What is a schilling?" the man asked.

"A second baseman," Charley replied. (Chuck Schilling played second base for the Boston Red Sox that year.)

Another time, Pete went with the neighbors to a Boston doubleheader at Metropolitan Stadium.

A neighbor remarked to Dave that the Boston pitcher, Frank Sullivan, had been around a long time.

"Yes," piped up Pete, quoting from the back on one of his cards. "He made his debut with the Red Sox in 1956." That's the year Pete was born.

Nicollet Memories

Late one fall my father came home with one of the best presents I ever received. It was the fielder's glove that Rance Pless had used in 1955, the year in which he led all American Association batters with a .337 average.

George Brophy, the Millers' general manager, knew that my father had a young son. Pless, the Millers' third baseman, had left one of his well-worn gloves in his locker at the end of the season, and Brophy gave it to my father with instructions to pass it along to me. I used it all the way through junior high, senior high, and American Legion baseball, relacing it many times before it eventually gave out.

I saw my first organized baseball game at Nicollet Park in South Minneapolis and went with my father several times each year until the park gave way to the modern Metropolitan Stadium in Bloomington.

Years later, when an editor at The Minneapolis Tribune *asked if anyone had any features they were dying to write, I said I wanted to do something on the history of Nicollet Park. Everyone I interviewed had a favorite Nicollet Park anecdote, and the final story could have been much longer if space permitted.*

The story, "Nicollet Park: A Colorful Page in Baseball History," originally appeared in The Minneapolis Tribune *on November 6, 1966.*

A classy page was torn out of baseball history when Nicollet Park's 279-foot right field fence was ripped down.

It was 10 years ago this month that a beautiful concrete, glass, and brick bank went up where the soggy, foul, rotten, and wonderful Nicollet Park once stood on the one-half city block bounded by W. 31st Street and Nicollet and Blaisdell Avenues.

Baseball game at Nicollet Park, April 1954.
Photo by Swan-Gillis, from the Minnesota Historical Society

The year before that, on September 28, 1955, the old Minneapolis Millers won their first and only Little World Series in the final game played in the old matchbox.

Newspapers the next morning ran a large picture of the old park, filled beyond capacity, under the words: "Nicollet's Last and Greatest Hour."

But, in bars from Lake St. to Lake City and amusement rooms from Ada to Zumbrota, people old enough to remember and sentimental enough to care still talk about Joe Hauser's record of 69 home runs, Mike Kelley's dogs who used to scare hell out of opposing right fielders, and that marvelous month of May 1951, when a kid named Mays came to town.

People may like the Minnesota Twins, but there's no arguing the fact that they loved the Millers.

Dave Moore, WCCO TV's newscaster, tells of going over to Miller games from KUOM's studios on the University of Minnesota campus.

In the group of youthful broadcasters was Ray Christensen, now play-by-play man for the Minnesota Vikings and Minnesota Gopher basketball on WCCO radio.

"We used to sit out in the left field bleachers and then Christensen would start his play-by-play. We'd all groan and ask, 'Do you want to sit next to him?'

"There'd only be about 500 people in the park and you could hear him all over. It was really embarrassing," Moore said.

111

"I can still hear him say, 'Jack Cassini at the plate. Big number three on the back of his grey St. Paul Saints road uniform.'"

Christensen doesn't deny Moore's recollections. In fact, he sounds rather proud of them.

"There was a wonderful intimacy about that place," he said. "There really wasn't a bad seat. You could hear conversations among the players and even see their faces.

"And another thing you don't see anymore is that everybody knew all the batting averages and numbers of all the players. And you hated the opposition. Every player was your enemy."

Nicollet, the Millers, and the American Association had a certain definite class.

Any league that could boast the Toledo Mud Hens for 50 years had to have class.

From 1915 until 1952, league membership was fixed with the same eight teams. Railroads linked the eastern division teams from Louisville, Indianapolis, Toledo, and Columbus and the western cities of Milwaukee, Minneapolis, St. Paul, and Kansas City.

Nicollet Park was built in 1896, six years before the formation of the American Association.

Not long after the start of Association play, in a park known for many home runs, came baseball's shortest.

Fleet Andy Oyler, the Millers' shortstop, was batting in the late innings of a game played in a steady drizzle. Those were the days when it was unusual to use a half dozen baseballs per game.

The pitch was low and Oyler chopped at it, sending it straight down into the mud in front of home plate. As Oyler circled the bases, the pitcher and catcher appealed for help and the entire infield joined the search for the ball.

Oyler slid across home plate just seconds in front of the futile tag by the second baseman who had found the ball just 5½ feet from home plate. That's a record which may last forever.

It was in those early years that the Park saw one of its best brawls. Both teams were about to converge upon umpire Brick Owens when Pudge Heffelfinger, Yale's three-time All America guard from Minnesota, jumped onto the field and saved Owens by offering to take on both teams.

The Millers were perhaps as well known for their rhubarbs as home runs.

Halsey Hall, who allegedly sat at Abner Doubleday's right hand when the latter invented baseball, said that the Millers' most memorable riot occurred in St. Paul at old Lexington Park on July 4, 1929.

"The St. Paul pitcher covered first on a bunt and was spiked by our runner. The pitcher threw the ball at the runner and the Millers' first base coach decked the pitcher. Both benches emptied and it took 20 minutes to clear the field," Hall said.

"It was one of those holiday split doubleheaders, and there was a full house at Nicollet in the afternoon. But, like so many of those affairs, the afternoon game was peaceful."

In 1954, the Millers, under fiery Bill Rigney, had their largest enforced exodus.

Jim Constable was pitching for Minneapolis, Herb Score for Indianapolis, and Stan Landes was umpiring.

Early in the game, Score, the Association's all-time strikeout leader, hit a Miller batter with a fast ball.

Three innings later, Constable hit Score with a slow curve.

Landes, never a popular local figure, threw Constable out of the game for deliberately hitting Score.

Rigney charged onto the field and explained to Landes, loud enough to be heard in the Twin City Rapid Transit Stables across 31st St., that if Constable were planning to hit Score he wouldn't have done it with a slow curve.

Landes told Rigney that he didn't need to be lectured on the finer points of bean balling and ordered Rigney from the field. The Miller dugout jockies took after Landes and out went two more players.

"Why don't you throw them all out," asked Rigney, who was waiting around for the final act.

"That's not a bad idea," replied Landes and to the showers went the entire Miller team except for Chico Ibanez, a Spanish-speaking utility infielder who was taking a siesta in the right field bullpen.

The Mike Kelley era is probably the most talked about in Miller history. From 1928 through 1937 the Irishman made money and friends by doing a thriving business in re-tooling old ball players.

"He used to build his team around that right field fence," recalled George Brophy, Miller business manager and now assistant farm director of the Minnesota Twins.

"He'd take a strong left handed hitter and give him a full year of play where he'd hit 30 home runs and never have to chase a ball in right field. Then he'd send him back to the majors for cash and other players.

"He used to break even on expenses and gate receipts and make his profit selling players. Most of the guys he sold to the majors never did anything again after they left Minneapolis."

Brophy told of Nicollet's biggest crowd. "One day Mike got stiff and told the ushers not to close the gates. There were 15,216 people there that day in a park built for 8,500 if you could get the people to sit close enough together in the bleachers.

"They were sitting along the foul lines and when the umpires demanded that the fans get off the field, Mike invited some to sit in the dugout."

Hall contributed the tale of Kelley's big Dalmatians who used to wander onto the field and growl at opposing right fielders. One day, Hall said, a Milwaukee right fielder refused to chase a long fly because he was paralyzed with fright by the dogs.

Part of Nicollet's lore exists in the realm of "hard to believe and verify" anecdotes.

Some fans say they were there the day an anonymous Miller stole first. The story has it that the player bunted his way to first and stole second on the first pitch to the next batter.

Then, on the next pitch, he raced back to first while the befuddled catcher just held the ball and stared. Not even Hall could confirm that one.

Moore's favorite eyewitness account took place in the mid-30s when Bill Norman, Saints' left fielder, came for a high fly ball, looked up, stopped in his tracks, turned green, and passed out. He had swallowed his cud of chewing tobacco.

It was at Nicollet that a young outfielder named Ted Williams won the league batting title in 1938 with a .366 average and showed that he possessed an equally fearsome temper.

According to stories, he dropped a fly ball, picked it up, dropped it, picked it up, dropped it, picked it up, and threw it over the fence.

In 1951, the New York Giants, with whom the Millers had a working agreement, assigned Willie Mays to Minneapolis. In 35 games he collected 71 hits, 8 home runs, and 30 runs batted in and was hitting a torrid .477 when the Giants claimed him.

Giant owner Horace Stoneham bought space in the news-papers to explain Mays was necessary to any Giant title hopes and that he was sorry for the plight of the Millers. The Giants, with Mays, won the title on Bobby Thomson's home run against the Dodgers. The Millers, without Mays, barely made the first division.

In the Little World Series of 1955, the Miller pitching hero was big Allan Worthington, who won three games and saved the final and last game at Nicollet. The Millers set a league record with 241 homers that year. Ten different players hit 12 or more home runs. The team batting average was .281 with seven players over .300. The American League had two .300 hitters in 1966.

To the players, Nicollet meant inadequate dressing facilities to be shared equally with the rats and termites. There were holes in the dressing room walls and the floor was wavy where the foundation had shifted since the park was built.

To the fans, it meant slivers from the wooden seats, gloves left on the field, autographs, and knothole days when 10 cents or a returned foul ball was good for one bleacher seat. It also meant the ushers who offered you tickets in exchange for foul balls and hinted strongly that you'd be wise to take the tickets.

To the press, it meant the wonderful press box built for the 1939 All-Star game. The facilities were first class, but you had to stand and lean forward to see the field.

To the management, it meant trouble with fire and police officials about inadequate exits into Nicollet Avenue traffic. It meant a constant duel with owners of Nicollet Avenue businesses about broken windows caused by pop-fly home runs over the 40-foot right field screen.

"We had so many windows broken in the President Cafe and Johnson's Appliances that only Lloyd's of London would insure us by the time we left," said Brophy.

"I remember that we were never too worried about a fire because the wood was so rotten that it wouldn't burn."

There were no parking facilities and homeowners in the area constantly complained about cars parked in front of their homes.

Opposing managers used to stall until 6 p.m. on Sundays because of a city ordinance against any inning starting after that time. Pop bottles and rented cushions used to greet any opposing manager who dared to change pitchers at 5:45 p.m. in the fourth inning.

Years later someone checked and no ordinance was found.

Two years before the team left, the ground crew, just for the heck of it, measured the distance from home plate to first base and found that Nicollet was no ordinary ballpark even in that simple respect. It turns out that for all of those years the distance had been only 88 instead of 90 feet.

In 1956, the Millers moved to Metropolitan Stadium and remained there until the Twins arrived in 1961. But for most fans, the thrill and flare of minor league baseball left when they killed old Nicollet.

On the Road with the Twins

When I took over the baseball beat for The Minneapolis Tribune *in the late 1960s, I was reasonably well prepared for covering the games but equally unprepared for what went on off the field.*

The Twins were scheduled to open the 1968 baseball season on the road against the Washington Senators. As the Twins prepared to fly to Washington, D.C., there was concern about whether the airport would be open and whether the city could host baseball. Just days earlier, on April 4, 1968, Civil Rights leader Martin Luther King Jr. had been assassinated. Riots broke out in more than 100 U.S. cities, and some 20,000 protestors took to the streets in the nation's capital and quickly overwhelmed the Washington police force. With riots moving within two blocks of the White House, President Lyndon Johnson dispatched 13,600 federal troops to restore order.

The Twins and the accompanying Minnesota press had both a police and military escort from the airport to our downtown hotel. We could see numerous fires as a blanket of smoke spread over the city.

At breakfast I told Tony Oliva I had never seen anything like it before.

"I have," he said, and he described the days when Fidel Castro was taking power in Cuba.

For much less dramatic encounters, the lobby of the Roosevelt Hotel in New York was a particularly good place to find off-the-field stories. Visiting teams and athletes often stayed at the Roosevelt, and kids could be found lurking in the hotel lobby in search of autographs from their heroes.

After sweeping the Senators in the two-game series to open the 1968 season, the Twins headed to New York for a two-game series against the New York Yankees. The following story, entitled "Autograph Hunter's Who's Who," appeared in The Minneapolis Tribune *on April 13, 1968.*

NEW YORK, N.Y. — What do Richie Allen, Bob Gibson, Frank Robinson, Mickey Mantle, Luis Aparicio, Jim Bunning, and Tim McCarver have in common?

"Those fellows are bad," agreed the boys of Taft High School in Manhattan, all of whom appear to be majoring in autographs. "They'd rather give you their blood than their autograph."

"We got 'em all," said Bob, the 15-year-old leader of the group of lads playing foot hockey by the door of the Roosevelt Hotel Friday afternoon.

"We're out of school today," one of the boys said. "It's Good Friday. You don't think we'd skip school for this sort of thing?" the boy continued in a voice that told you they would.

"Cool it," another warned. "The guy's taking notes. Act sophisticated."

"Put in that not all the guys are jerks," a lad requested. "Most of the really good guys are the superstars. Harmon Killebrew's great. So are Ron Santo, Ernie Banks, Al Kaline, Roberto Clemente, Brooks Robinson, and Roger Maris.

"Then there's guys like Tom Tresh. He'll sign anything."

While some players don't like to sign autographs, some live in fear of the boys, they bragged. "You should see Lou Brock," one said with a laugh. "He runs away from us. We chased him for two blocks through the airport one day."

The boys, who say they are the best, don't restrict their hunting to baseball. "We get all the professional sports," Ken said. "Do you know any of the Minnesota North Stars? Tell Bob Woytowich that Kenny in New York said to say hello. He'll know what you mean."

The boys send to equipment manufacturers for glossy pictures of the players and have the players autograph the pictures.

They can tell you in about the time it takes to write Jackie Robinson, the New York headquarters of every professional team and whether the doorman is friendly.

Constant trading takes place among the collectors. The bidding on an original Babe Ruth is up to $20, a Lou Gehrig, $50.

Bob said his gang will stop at nothing to get autographs. "We go on planes, in buses, on trains, in locker rooms, and dugouts. You got to learn not to take it personally when you get tossed out of a place. Otherwise, you might get discouraged. We're going to Cooperstown this year to get all the old-timers."

Despite the reluctance of Mantle to part with his name, Bob claims "about 50 Mantles."

"The trick is if he's going to sign just one or two, to get an old lady to go up to him. He'll always sign for her. That's how I got most of my Mantles."

The boys aren't the only ones who bother players at New York hotels.

"See that redhead there?" Bob asked. "She goes everywhere we go. I bet she knows every player in the league."

"Does she collect autographs, too?" an innocent asked.

"Autographs!" the group chorused. "That's tremendous!"

The Twins will take on the New York Yankees in a battle of undefeated teams at Yankee Stadium this afternoon. Bob's gang and the redhead will attend.

Halsey Hall, Burning up the Airwaves

Each year when the Minnesota Twins Hall of Fame ballot arrives in the mail, the first name I check is Halsey Hall's. I'll continue to do it until he's elected.

Long before he joined the Twins original radio broadcast team, Hall was on his way to legendary status. He had covered sports for years as a reporter for *The Minneapolis Tribune, St. Paul Pioneer Press*, and *The Minneapolis Star*. He broadcast Minneapolis Millers minor league baseball games for years and provided color commentary on University of Minnesota football broadcasts. By the 1960s, he was an institution on the Minnesota sports scene.

Somebody made a great decision when they installed Hall as a member of the Twins first broadcast team in 1961, along with Ray Scott and Bob Wolfe, who left after one year to open a slot for Herb Carneal. Whereas Scott and Wolfe were new to the market, Halsey was a familiar voice and a true character.

The first time I met Halsey I asked him how he got started in newspaper writing.

"The profession wasn't so highly regarded at that time," he explained, "so I wrote to my parents and told them I'd found employment playing piano in a bawdy house, and that seemed to satisfy them."

I covered the Twins as the beat reporter for *The Minneapolis Tribune* in 1968 and 1969. I couldn't get enough of Halsey's stories, and there was nothing he liked better than a new audience.

Jet travel in those years was a little different. Rather than leave directly from the terminal gates, we usually walked onto the tarmac and up a set of stairs to our charter jet. On an early road trip that started in Chicago, I followed Halsey up the steps. He wore a rumpled trench coach and carried a large Dayton's shopping bag. Climbing the steps was never easy for Halsey, and I noticed a distinct tinkling sound coming from the shopping bag.

Seated across from him, I asked him what was in the bag.

"My books," he said with a smile. "Never can do enough research about the opponents."

I suggested that his books sounded as if they were made from glass, not paper.

"Ah, that," he confided. "Just a small amount of the juice of the barley."

It made no sense to me why someone as smart as Halsey would bring booze from a high-tax state like Minnesota to a low-cost alcohol market like Chicago, and I told him as much.

Leaning across the aisle and lowering his voice, he patiently explained. "Davy, me boy. What you say is undoubtedly true, but you never know when you might run into a local election." (He was referring to local ordinances that existed in many communities banning the sale of alcohol on election day.)

My favorite Halsey memories center on Chicago and New York.

Near the beginning of a nearly two-week road trip, we were playing the White Sox in a doubleheader. In those days the press boxes were connected to other major league press boxes via Western Union ticker tape. The small black box chattered constantly, rolling out an uninterrupted half-inch-wide ribbon of half-inning scores, pitching changes, and home runs.

During the course of an afternoon, shreds of tape littered a portion of the press box. The broadcast booths had their own tapes, adding a sound of familiarity to each broadcast. By the late innings of the doubleheader nightcap, the tape could be ankle deep, and it often clung to the shoes of broadcasters like a piece of toilet paper.

Halsey smoked cigars. Constantly.

He held the cigar in the same right hand he used to keep score, and he never put it down, pausing only occasionally to shake off the growing ashes.

By the seventh inning of the second game in Chicago, the combination of the ticker tape and ashes was incendiary. In short order, white smoke was pouring out of the visiting broadcast booth, and both dugouts emptied to see what had caught the attention of the entire crowd. Luckily, the damage was minor. Halsey had burned a hole in the cuffs of his pants and in his sport coat. Carneal and Merle Harmon, Halsey's broadcast partners, never missed a pitch as they helped stamp out the fire.

After the game, players were interviewing reporters, trying to find out what had happened in the press box.

Minnesota's veteran backup catcher, Jerry Zimmerman, had an observation that made all the newspapers the next day. "That Halsey's quite a guy," he said. "He's the only person I know who could turn an ordinary sport coat into a blazer in nothing flat."

When the team visited New York to play the Yankees, the Twins stayed at the Roosevelt Hotel, not far from Grand Central

Halsey Hall (right) with Herb Carneal and Merle Harmon, circa 1962.
Minnesota Historical Society

Station. On occasion, Twins public relations director Tom Mee would pass the word that he was hosting a dinner after a game at the Cattleman Restaurant, a short walking distance from the Roosevelt.

Most of the restaurant was a flight down from street level in a series of smaller rooms, all pretty much the same.

Halsey—who never turned down a chance to attend a dinner with reporters, broadcasters, or front-office personnel—was quick to figure out which dinners were hosted and which ones were on our own. If the Twins were buying, Halsey was happy to order generously from the bar menu. If we were on our own, he would purchase an initial drink and refill it the rest of the evening from a pocket flask that he had been using since the days of Prohibition.

One night at the Cattleman, Halsey excused himself to use the men's room, and the remaining ten of us decided to have some fun with him. We told our server to bring the bill to Halsey while we all hid out of sight.

Slowly, Halsey made his way back to the room he thought was ours. It was after 2 a.m. and the place was rapidly emptying. Not seeing his friends, he shook his head and tried another room. Then another. Nobody familiar.

Finally, our server spotted him and explained that since the hour was late, his friends had gone back to the hotel, but not before they assured the server that the white-haired gentleman would be handling the bill, which was in the neighborhood of $300, a small fortune at the time.

Looking at the bottom line, Halsey clearly was shaken. "My good lady," he stammered, "there has to be a mistake here."

She did her best to continue the charade, but eventually Mee stepped forward to put Halsey out of his discomfort.

At another late dinner at the Cattleman, Halsey spent most of the evening complaining about the size of his room at the Roosevelt. He also didn't like the fact that it was next to the elevator and he could hear the bell every time a car stopped on his floor. With each drink he consumed, the bell got louder and his room got smaller.

On the way back to the hotel, Mee said he would talk to the front desk about getting Halsey a better room.

Hotels don't have their first team working at 2:45 a.m., but the young desk clerk was doing his best in a language that clearly was both new and difficult for him. Mee did most of the talking while Halsey listened.

Finally, after little progress, the desk clerk said, "And how big a room does the gentleman require?"

Halsey, recognizing a spot for a one-liner, interrupted the conversation.

"Well, for Christ's sakes," he slurred, "the gentleman at least needs a room big enough to fall down in."

An R-Rated Fish Story

Halsey Hall's stories were so well known among his fellow travelers that they had shorthand names.

As the writers covering the Twins prepared for our first East Coast road trip of the 1968 season, several of the veteran writers and club officials urged me to seek out Halsey and have him tell me the "Boston fish story."

After landing at Logan Airport, I climbed on the bus and grabbed a seat across the aisle from Halsey. I told him that I had been instructed to ask him about the Boston fish story.

He smiled as he rapidly sorted through his repertoire. But first, he needed to qualify his audience.

"Do you like fish?"

Most of the fish I had eaten in my South Minneapolis home were about four inches long and came twelve to a box. Somehow I suspected he was looking for something more global.

"I like walleye, sunnies, crappies, and smelt," I told him, rapidly naming all the different fish I had ever tasted.

"Not those fish. Those are Minnesota fish. I'm talking about ocean fish."

Unsure how to count "Chicken of the Sea," I admitted that my experience with sea fish was sadly lacking.

"No problem," he said. "When we get to Baltimore you can try crab cakes, and Boston has just about everything. Great New England fresh lobster, red snapper, jumbo shrimp—you name it. But the story they're talking about has to do with another great fish in this region. It seems there was a businessman who was going to be in Boston for several days. Some of his friends gave him tips on where to eat and what to ask for. They said if he had just one chance to order fresh seafood, he needed to try the scrod.

"Time got away from him and he was in his last night in Boston when he remembered his friends' advice. He hailed a cab outside his hotel and decided to ask the driver for a recommendation. 'My good fellow,' he said, 'can you tell me where a gentleman can get scrod in this town?'

"The cabbie paused a minute before replying.

"'Being in this business I bet I've been asked that question a thousand times, but this is the first time I've heard it in the pluperfect subjunctive!'"

A Great Quote

I had relatively little to do with Twins owner Calvin Griffith during the two years I covered the team for *The Minneapolis Tribune*, but he was almost always available if I simply stopped by his office in the bowels of Metropolitan Stadium and asked to talk. As long as it wasn't naptime, I could usually get in to see him within a few minutes.

Interviews with Calvin often lasted longer than planned because he would digress into sundry items from his vast memories of growing up in the Washington Senators organization.

Once, when the Twins were in salary negotiations with star outfielder Tony Oliva, I stopped by to see Griffith for a progress report. What followed was a fascinating conversation about the history of the Senators as it related to Cuban baseball players. Imagine how history might have been changed if the Senators had been able to agree to terms with a promising athlete named Fidel Castro.

Although I was looking for just a single quote on the negotiations with Oliva, I got the entire history of Oliva's signing and the way they got him out of Cuba by using his brother's passport.

Calvin talked about how Oliva was a natural-born hitter who came to the Twins with little idea of how to catch a ball. One thing led to another, and soon Calvin was quizzing me.

"Did you ever hear of Carlos Paula?" he asked, probing my knowledge of the Senators' history.

Reaching back to my baseball card collecting days, I said, "Cuban outfielder who played for you guys in the mid fifties."

"That's right, but do you remember his most famous play?"

He had me there, but I knew I was about to learn.

"Paula was a lot like Oliva," Calvin said. "We liked to get his bat in the lineup, but he was a terrible fielder. One day in Washington we had him in the outfield and a guy hit a shot right at him. It took one hard hop right between his legs. When he turned around to play it off the fence, it went between his legs again. Two fielding errors on the same play. Never saw anything like it."

Nearing deadline, I reminded Calvin that Oliva, unlike Paula, had built himself into one of the best defensive outfielders in the league at the same time he was winning batting titles.

"Can you give me anything for the record on how your negotiations are going?" I asked.

"I'll tell you this much," he said. "Oliva's English is bad enough to keep him out of the United States Army, but every time he sits down to talk contract with me, he sounds like Winston Churchill."

I didn't have all the facts, but I had my quote, and sometimes that was all you wanted from Calvin.

I decided to give up the Twins beat after the 1969 season. I was tired of spending more than a hundred days each year away from home while earning $6,500 a year.

132

Billy Martin's firing was the last sports story I covered for *The Minneapolis Tribune*, and once again the story led me into Griffith's office. A "Bring Billy Back" rebellion was under way among Twins fans, and Griffith was facing enormous pressure to reconsider his decision.

Sometimes, when under pressure, Griffith was known to misuse large words. Usually the media would substitute the intended word. But this was my last story, and I wrote it as he gave it to me. Here's how the conversation went:

With Tony Oliva at Twins Spring Training, 1968

"Calvin, you're under a lot of pressure to reconsider and bring Billy back. Can you give us any indication of what you're thinking?"

"I'm getting a lot of advice from a lot of different people, and I'm not ready yet to announce what we are planning to do. But when we get to that point, I can assure you, we aren't going to do anything rational."

The Killer Speaks

One of the first players I met as a major league baseball writer was Harmon Killebrew.

"You must be the new guy," he said to me as I stepped onto Orlando's Tinker Field during spring training in February 1968. "I'm Harmon Killebrew."

As if I or anyone else didn't know. But that was Harmon, already a thirteen-year veteran on his way to the National Baseball Hall of Fame in Cooperstown, New York.

Other sportswriters had said that Harmon was probably the nicest guy on the Twins but rarely good for a memorable quote. Although that was generally true, he was always open to a conversation and never said no to an interview request.

Very early in my days on the Twins beat, I saw that Harmon received more fan mail than almost the rest of the team combined. Such is the fame and attention that follow a man who is on his way to hitting five hundred home runs. One day, hours before a home game at Metropolitan Stadium, I saw him sitting at his locker signing a series of Topps baseball cards and patiently putting them back into a self-addressed stamped envelope. Each card carried the patented perfect Killebrew signature, every letter legible.

"Do you answer every one?" I asked.

"I try to," he said. "It may take me a while, but I try to get to all of them, especially the ones with the return envelopes."

"Are they all just requests for autographs?" I asked.

"Most of them. But I get a lot of notes and letters too."

In my mind, a story was starting to take shape, so I asked him if I could take a look.

"Here's a stack I just finished," he said. "Help yourself."

Harmon Killebrew at Twins Spring Training, 1964.
Minnesota Historical Society

I took them home with me after the game that night and started to read the notes. The majority of them were written in pencil on lined paper. At least two thirds of them proclaimed Harmon to be their favorite player. A number of them referenced games they had seen either in person or on television.

Many made observations that didn't call for a direct response.

"I bet you were happy to get Dean Chance in a trade. . . ."

"My dad says there is not a chance you will answer this. . . ."

"My friend says Mickey Mantle can hit a ball farther than you can, but. . . ."

One, I recall, posed a question that seemed to beg for a response. "My mom and dad say that if I want to grow up to be able to hit like you, I need to eat my vegetables. I hate vegetables. What do you think?"

At the park the next day I approached Harmon as he waited his turn at the batting cage.

"What did you think of my mail?" he asked.

"It was fun reading. Very informative. Do you remember the one from the kid who asked about eating his vegetables?"

"Sure."

"Did you answer that one?"

"Absolutely."

"Do you mind telling me what you said?"

"Not at all. I told him to eat his vegetables."

He then stepped into the batting cage and demonstrated the importance of a balanced diet by lining three straight pitches into the left-field seats.

Killebrew's version of batting practice differed from that of the other players. Everyone else took seven swings and laid down a bunt on the final pitch. Harmon took eight full swings. His job was to hit home runs, and he did it better than any other player in Twins history. He retired without ever laying down a sacrifice bunt.

Years later, my wife and I attended a seminar at which the speaker talked about the mistake we make in drilling people to improve their weaknesses instead of allowing them to focus on their exceptional talents.

"If you spend all your life trying to improve your weaknesses," he promised, "you will die with a lot of strong weaknesses."

One example the speaker used was Babe Ruth, who hit 714 career home runs without a single sacrifice bunt. My wife and I looked at each other, smiled, and said at the same time, "Harmon Killebrew."

During the years I covered the Twins, the *Tribune* started a new feature, "The Monday Morning Quarterback," written by Paul Foss. Foss ran a local printing company and was a friend of the publisher. The players usually paid little attention to what was written about them, but Harmon saw me at the batting cage one day and asked if I had read what Foss had written about him in that morning's paper. It was just one line: "Is Harmon having trouble with the curve ball?" Harmon, usually the most mild-mannered player on the team, clearly was miffed.

That night he hit a home run, and I was among the reporters who gathered around his locker after the game.

"What pitch did you hit on the homer?" one of the reporters asked.

"I'm not really sure," Harmon replied.

I couldn't help myself. "From the press box it looked like a curve ball," I offered.

Harmon, looking up from unlacing his shoes, smiled at me and said, "Yeah, it was definitely a curve ball."

In fact, I think his next five home runs came off curve balls.

Most casual fans will tell you that Killebrew played his entire career with the Washington Senators/Minnesota Twins. But not quite.

He ended his career in 1975 with the Kansas City Royals, where he hit .199 with 14 home runs in 106 games. For the aging slugger, it was an agonizing limp toward retirement.

In a radio interview I once asked him how he knew it was time to retire. He said:

I was playing for the Royals, and not helping them much or having much fun. We were in Anaheim to play the

Angels. It was a long time before the start of the game and the gates must have just opened. I was looking for a bat in the rack at the end of the dugout and I could hear some kids down at the other end.

"Who's that old guy?" a smaller kid said to an older one.

"That's Harmon Killebrew," the bigger kid said.

"Is he any good?" the younger kid said.

And the older kid said, "He used to be."

Harmon Killebrew retired at the end of that season and was elected to the Hall of Fame in 1984. He saved one of his best stories for his induction speech. He reminisced about growing up in Idaho and playing a variety of sports. One day, he recalled, he was playing a game of football in his front yard. His mother saw the damage that was being done to their lawn and shared her concern with Harmon's father.

"Honey," he said, "we're not raising grass. We're raising boys."

Who Does That Humphrey Think He Is?

Billy Martin was a reporter's dream. Every day was filled with explosive possibilities.

Martin's first major league managing job was with the Twins in 1969. He was fired despite winning the title in the inaugural season of the American League Western Division.

I spent a fair amount of time with Billy as he prepared for his managerial debut, and it was clear that things were going to be radically different from the previous year under Cal Ermer, a loyal member of the Calvin Griffith organization.

There was a long-standing adage in baseball that players, not managers, won games. Martin was not its author.

Billy was determined to put his mark on the Twins. They were going to run more. They were going to pitch inside. They were going to take the extra base. And, starting with the manager, they would never back down.

They also would establish new traditions while holding nothing sacred.

We got our first preview early in spring training at Tinker Field in Orlando.

One of the Twins' greatest fans was Hubert Humphrey. As a U.S. senator from Minnesota, he befriended a number of players and team officials. He was proud that the Washington Senators had moved to Minnesota in 1961, and he was an unapologetic fan from the start. He also knew the publicity value of being seen with high-profile athletes. It was not uncommon for him to attend several games during the year, so it was no surprise to hear that he was going to visit the team in Orlando.

Because he was a former vice president of the United States, he traveled with tight security and a bevy of political reporters.

Ordinarily Martin was pleased to see a large number of reporters. He was good with the media and he knew it. But on this day the reporters were oblivious to Martin, and he was seething.

"Who the hell does he think he is?" he sneered, gesturing at Humphrey, who was being photographed giving batting tips to Twins slugger Harmon Killebrew.

"He's the former vice president of the United States," someone suggested.

"I don't give a crap who he is," Martin hissed. "Let him get his pictures and get the hell off my field."

That side of Martin came up again on our first trip into Washington to play the expansion Senators.

Billy knew a good story angle. This was the first meeting between the team that had left Washington against the expansion team of the same name. A student of baseball, Billy thought he had a good grasp of the situation.

The Twins arrived a day early and scheduled a workout to check out the mostly unfamiliar ballpark. The Senators had worked out just before the Twins.

Martin loved attention, and there were dozens of local and national reporters on site. Trouble is, they paid no attention to Martin. They were gathered around the new Senators manager, hanging on his every word. It mattered little to Martin that the object of their attention was a guy named Ted Williams.

Hubert Humphrey with Bob Allison, Cal Ermer, and Calvin Griffith, Twins Spring Training, March 1968.
From the Hubert H. Humphrey Photograph Collection, Minnesota Historical Society

As Williams did interview after interview, Martin retreated to his manager's office adjacent to the Twins clubhouse. Arno Goethel, the Twins reporter for the St. Paul newspapers, and I went with him.

"Did you see those assholes follow him around? Every time he opened his mouth there was someone there with a microphone."

It was clear that Billy was just getting started.

"You know," he confided, "Williams wasn't half the player Mickey [Mantle] was."

Hubert Humphrey signing baseball for Billy Martin, then the Twins third-base coach, March 1968.
From the Hubert H. Humphrey Photograph Collection, Minnesota Historical Society

Arno and I looked at each other to see if either of us was taking notes.

"Williams was a great hitter, but Mickey was a complete player. He could do it all. Field, run, throw, hit with power.

"In his entire career did you ever see Ted slide hard into second base to break up a double play?"

Finally Arno, who had been on the beat nearly a decade longer than I, spoke.

"Billy," he said, "can we write this?"

"I don't give a shit," he said. "It's the truth."

Arno may have been more experienced, but he was no match in a footrace. I was already on my third paragraph when he reached the press box. Writing as fast as I could, I finished the story and ran outside to find a cab to the nearest Western Union office.

By the time I got back to my hotel, I already had a message to call my sports editor, Larry Batson.

"This is great stuff," he said. "We're going big with it."

When Arno and I got to the ballpark the next morning, we were met by a frantic Art Fowler, Billy's closest friend and one of the Twins' pitching coaches.

"Skip wants to see you guys. Right away."

To say that Martin was livid does little justice to the situation. He wanted blood.

"I thought you guys were my friends," he shouted.

"What did we do?" Goethel asked.

"You've got to be kidding. I got my first call at the hotel about six this morning. The *Washington Post* is all over me. Every radio and TV station in town is after me to talk about Williams."

Ordinarily, Martin loved media attention, but this was no ordinary morning.

At shortly after ten o'clock each night, duplicated copies of all locally produced stories for the Minneapolis and St. Paul morning papers were shipped via pneumatic tube to the offices of the Associated Press. About midnight, the stories moved on the national wire service into newsrooms across the nation. Martin's quotes were the lead item.

Goethel took advantage of a lull in Martin's ravings to explain.

"Billy, we stood right here and asked you if we could write this stuff. We knew it would be a big story and that's why we asked you if we could run it, and you said yes."

The explanation worked.

"You're right."

And then he elaborated a set of ground rules, which we followed right up until the day he was fired.

"Here's the deal. You guys are going to be practically living with me for a whole season. I'm probably going to say a lot of outrageous things. When I do, you have to tell me. I'm probably going to tell you to go ahead and write it, but you got to let me know."

A Salute and a Vote

In a most uncharacteristic display of spending, *The Minneapolis Tribune* editors decided to send someone to cover the 1968 Olympic Games in Mexico City. With the Minnesota Twins out of the American League pennant race, it was clear that I was going to be available for general assignment duty in October.

"Ever been to Mexico?" sports editor Larry Batson asked me during the final week of baseball season. "We've been thinking of sending someone to cover the Olympics. We'll get all the results and stuff from the wire services, so we need someone to provide the local color. Lots of features. I know you got married in the middle of the baseball season. You can take Linda with you. Call it a working honeymoon."

It was the best sales job I was to hear in my five years at the newspaper. Two weeks in a foreign country on an expense account that would cover up to fourteen dollars per day. Frommer would approve.

Mexico City had been a surprise choice to host the Olympics. The country was massively underdeveloped and suffering from social and political unrest. Not that the rest of the world was much better. The United States was bogged down in what seemed like an endless war in Vietnam, and its major cities had been on fire that summer. Russia had recently invaded Czechoslovakia, and Israel was at odds with the entire Arab world.

Two weeks before the start of the Olympics, some three hundred students had been shot and killed by government forces at a demonstration in Mexico City. When we flew in, it was obvious that the country wanted to make its visitors feel safe and welcome. It had stationed soldiers armed with Uzis about every twenty feet at the airport. It was of little comfort that most of them looked as if they were several years shy of their first shave.

The Mexican government had built two villages in preparation for the Olympics. The first, for the athletes, was in the central city. Ours, Villa Coapa, was to be turned into affordable, low-rise housing after the Olympics. It was on the outskirts of Mexico City, about fifteen miles from most of the events. It was home to journalists, minor officials, participants in the concurrent cultural Olympics, and just about everyone else connected with the games. Security was tight, and armed guards were everywhere.

We were staying on the fourth floor of a new stucco building that had narrow staircases and no elevator. The housing was so new that the plaster wasn't even dry.

Prior to 1968 I was much more familiar with Norwegian than Spanish, and language challenges dominated major parts of every day. We had a spacious bedroom unit and shared a bathroom with a reporter from Africa who spoke no English. Together, we shared a few common French words.

Mexico may have been the first Olympic host to maximize the concept of what was to become sports marketing. At numerous locations throughout the compound there were State Fair types of booths offering a chocolate drink called Ovalmaltina. A prominently located building offered products by a company called Adidas. Their shoes and warmups were far more stylish than anything we had seen in the United States at the time, and they must have sold products to representatives of every country covering the games. It was a brilliant marketing ploy.

By the time we checked in and found the way to our unit, it was already late evening and time to crash for the night. The literature had mentioned nothing about the mosquitoes. As Minnesotans, we thought we had written the book on mosquitoes, but our mosquitoes were to these mosquitoes what a Piper Cub is to a Boeing 747. Taking towels in hand, my wife and I stood on opposite sides of the bed and went to war. After about twenty minutes, our deft touch and superior firepower turned the tide. In time, we were confident that we had annihilated the entire colony. Exhausted, we fell asleep.

Early in the night, reinforcements must have arrived from under the door and from the corner where the window didn't quite line up with the wall. Tired of fighting, we crawled under the sheets and fell asleep. When we awoke the next morning, Linda's left eye was the size of Wisconsin.

Even with sunglasses, it was impossible to hide the damage. Everywhere we went in the village, people, in dozens of languages, wanted to know what had happened. Linda, doing her best mosquito impression, tried to re-create the incident. Most of the men merely looked at me, smiled, slapped their right fist into the left hand, and laughed appreciatively. We were still several years away from the arrival of sensitivity training.

At breakfast every morning in the cafeteria, only two things looked familiar to us young Minnesotans. We virtually lived on glazed donuts for those two weeks (they were delicious), but it took some negotiating to survive the egg station. The fry cooks were inexperienced, and we learned together. Five seconds is a little short of the time it takes to fry an egg. By communicating that we preferred our eggs "over," we were able to double the cooking cycle, but we were never able to win that battle completely.

We tried our best to experience the local cuisine. Lunches and dinners began with a basket of fried chips and a dipping bowl of hot chili sauce. What was later to become a staple of any Super Bowl party was new to us in Mexico City in 1968.

One of the first Olympic events we attended was a track-and-field competition. Much had been written prior to the games about how the athletes might perform at the city's high altitude, but no one was prepared to see American Ralph Boston shatter the Olympic and world long-jump record by nearly two feet.

The high-jump finals took place a short distance from our seats, and all but the veteran track-and-field writers were astounded to see an American named Dick Fosbury win the event by launching himself over the bar backward in what would soon be known as the "Fosbury Flop."

We wanted to see the U.S. basketball team in action, and we quickly learned that if we wanted anything more than a sheet showing last names and total points scored, we were on our own. Over the next week, my wife, Linda, became an expert in noting rebounds, steals, blocks, and assists as we supplied our own stats to complement the game stories I was writing and carrying to the Mexican version of Western Union for transmission back to Minneapolis.

Wanting to explore the tension between the Soviet Union and Czechoslovakia, we signed up for a water polo meet between the two nations. The Czechs, who had no match for the Soviet tanks, were dominant in the pool in a violent game that saw the waters turn red with Soviet blood.

We missed the signature event of the games, when American sprinters John Carlos and Tommie Smith raised their fists in a black power salute during the playing of the "Star Spangled Banner." We most likely were on a bus because that's where we spent much of our time. The Mexican organizing committee had done a great job of lining up state-of-the art buses to transport journalists and other officials the great distances between events. That fleet, far superior to the local public transportation, proved to be very popular.

One night, after the completion of women's gymnastics events, we boarded a bus clearly marked "Villa Coapa." Soon, every seat and the aisles were jammed far beyond capacity. The driver expertly jockeyed the bus through traffic and onto one of Mexico City's busiest streets. It was clear that we were heading away from the central city, and a few people began to shout their objections. Chaos reigned, and the driver was the target. Very few of the riders had any sort of credential. We may have been the only journalists on the media bus. The hour was late, and they just wanted to be in their downtown hotels.

Stopping the bus in the middle of a six-lane street, the driver stood and shouted for attention: This was a media bus headed for Villa Coapa. The masses begged to differ. This bus was going to the downtown hotels, they insisted. It was a classic stalemate.

With hundreds of cars honking at us, the driver announced that we were going to vote. How many in favor of Villa Coapa? He got a few tentative votes. How many in favor of downtown Mexico City? An overwhelming majority. With a shrug of the shoulders he climbed back into the driver's seat, edged his way left through three lanes of backed-up traffic, drove over the median—to the thunderous approval of most of the riders—and headed for the downtown hotels.

It was nearly two o'clock in the morning when we got back to our compound. Although it may have been a breakdown of the Olympic transportation system, it was a clearly an optimistic sign for the future of Mexican democracy.

Part III

The Huddle, and Beyond

It's the *Sports Huddle* with Sid and Dave

As soon as my wife, Linda, and I decided that I was going to start my own public relations firm, I heard about and signed up for a "Getting Into Business" course offered by the Service Corps of Retired Executives (SCORE).

This was 1981, long before the advent of PowerPoint. After introductions, the first speaker for the course opened with a daunting statistic, illuminated via overhead projector, about the failure rate of new businesses: eighty percent will fail in the first year; ninety percent will be gone in less than two years.

Although I was no math major, it dawned on me that there was an outside chance that my new PR firm might not make it. I needed a backup plan—something that might provide supplemental income and/or a possible alternative to my first choice.

Over the years I had gotten to know a number of people at WCCO Radio: Phil Lewis, Clayt Kauffman, By Napier, Curtis Beckman, and Larry Haeg Jr. Although I had no background in radio, I had worked at WCCO TV and *The Minneapolis Tribune*, and I was still doing freelance work for United Press International. I thought all that experience might be enough to qualify me for at least an audition tape session, and I was right.

I left the audition with a promise that the station would consider me if it needed another hand on something such as color analysis for high school tournament broadcasts.

On a Thursday about three weeks later, I fielded a call from the WCCO program director, By Napier.

"If you're still interested, I might have something for you," he said. "Do you ever listen to that show that Sid Hartman does on Sunday mornings with Chuck Lillegren?"

"You mean the *Sports Huddle?*" I said. "Sure, I listen just about every week."

"Do you think you could do that show?"

By now I was getting excited. I thought Sid was leaving.

It turned out to be Lillegren who was leaving the WCCO weekend shift to move to weekdays. For whatever reason, Lillegren decided he didn't want to sacrifice his weekends to come in for a show that ran from only 10:05 to 10:30 on Sunday mornings.

Without hesitation I said I'd be happy to do the *Sports Huddle,* and I asked Napier what he had in mind.

"Why don't you plan to be down here about 9:45 or so, and we'll see how it sounds."

"What day?" I countered.

"Sunday, of course."

"Which Sunday?"

"This Sunday."

Lillegren had been wanting to get off the *Sports Huddle* for nearly a month by this point, and knowing that nothing would happen until he forced the issue, he scheduled himself to be out of town for that weekend. The station needed a quick fix, if not a permanent repair.

Napier and I never got around to discussing compensation or any other terms.

I arrived at the station's front door at 9:40 on the morning of my scheduled debut. It was locked.

I couldn't use my cell phone—they wouldn't be invented for about another decade—so I raced down the block to the Minneapolis Athletic Club. I knew there were some courtesy phones at the back of the lobby for the convenience of club members. I wasn't a member, but I needed to use a phone. And fast.

Someone answered at the WCCO switchboard.

"Hi, this is Dave Mona and I was just at the door and it's locked," I explained.

"Yes," she said, "the door is locked every Sunday."

"But I need to get in. I'm supposed to be on with Sid in about fifteen minutes."

"Are you a guest?"

"Trust me. Lillegren isn't going to be there, and I need to get in to be on the air in less than fifteen minutes."

She agreed to meet me at the door and let me in. By now it was 9:55. My radio debut was ten minutes away. I headed back to the studio.

I went to the same studio where I had done my audition tape. It was the only WCCO studio I knew. Where was everyone? I was in the wrong studio! Fortunately, an engineer, sitting out of sight behind the glass, recognized my plight and told me, "He doesn't do the show from that studio. Go out the door, turn right, and go in the first door on the right."

Relieved, I made my way into the small space where Sid and Chuck had worked for the almost four years that they did the *Sports Huddle* together. It was now 10:03, and the local news was ending. As the familiar *Sports Huddle* theme began, Sid entered the studio.

Here it comes, I knew—my pep talk.

"Do you know how to turn the microphones on?" he asked.

I had assumed that Sid had mastered the technological mysteries of radio during his first quarter century at the microphone.

"Don't worry," the disembodied engineer said. "I'll get you on the air."

The theme was winding down as Sid spoke once more.

"Nothing against you, David," he said, "but this isn't going to work. I'm going to ask them to cancel the show."

And that's when the "On the Air" button turned red.

That was the spring of 1981. In 2006 we celebrated our twenty-fifth anniversary, and Sid and I have done more than 1,300 shows together since that modest debut.

Inside the *Sports Huddle*

People often ask me how much preparation I do each week for the now two-and-a-half-hour *Sports Huddle*. It's a hard question to answer.

Sid and I arrive at the WCCO studios between 9 and 9:15 every Sunday morning. We rarely talk much about the show before we go on the air. The first thirty minutes are usually devoted to conversations with various coaches and managers. In recent years that rotation has been Twins managers Tom Kelly or Ron Gardenhire during the baseball season and Gopher coaches Tubby Smith and Tim Brewster in the fall and winter.

After the Twins left WCCO for another station in 2007, we filled the managers' slot with a series of interviews with high-profile guests, including Paul Molitor, Terry Steinbach, Kevin McHale, Fred Hoiberg, Doug Risebrough, Don Lucia, Brad Childress, Rick Spielman, and Joel Maturi, among others. Our ratings held steady, but it felt strange not talking to the Twins skipper during that time slot.

While Sid spends the first seven minutes of the show interviewing the manager or coach, I write out on a small sheet of paper some topics to discuss over the next two hours. The basic categories on the list never change: Twins, Vikings, Wild, Timberwolves, Gophers, and other. For each main category I add notes about who's been traded, demoted, or promoted; who's injured; who's hot and who's not. During one of the commercial breaks, I'll ask Sid what guests he has lined up.

Sid usually waits until studio coordinator Dave Schultz is fielding calls from listeners before he starts shouting phone numbers at him.

"Schultzie, Joel Maturi is going to call at 10:05. Keep that unlisted number open for him. Call Matt Birk at 10:30. Here's his phone

Me and Sid with Gophers basketball coach Clem Haskins at
the 1997 NCAA Men's Basketball Final Four

number. Randy Wittman said he'd call at 11:05. If he forgets, here's his number. The Twins said they'd get us Morneau, and Risebrough said he'd call if he got a chance. Did you get all that?"

"And don't forget to tell the Twins we don't want Denny Hocking." (The always-available Hocking is long gone, but he lingers in Sid's mind as the name of any guest the team tries to get us instead of the requested stars.)

Most of the numbers that Sid fires at the studio coordinators are right. On occasion he refers to his personal directory, which is the size of the Fridley phone book.

Our regular listeners sense when we are going to start taking phone calls. Even without prompting, our five incoming lines begin to fill and pretty much stay that way until we sign off at 11:57 a.m.

People often say that they tune in just to hear Sid hang up on callers who don't agree with him. In truth, Sid doesn't hang up on anybody. To accommodate as many callers as possible, we try to limit callers to a single question. If Sid disagrees with the direction of that question, his response will be short, sometimes personal, and to the point.

Several years ago a reasonable-sounding caller asked Sid why he was so rude to listeners. I sit about six feet away from him, and I could see that he was mulling the right answer.

"I don't think I'm rude to callers," he said. Looking straight at me, he implored, "Do you?"

"Of course you are. That's one of the reasons people listen. In this world of Minnesota nice, you give them something different."

For the remainder of that show, he thanked everyone for calling. Sometimes twice.

Thankfully, before listeners could adjust to a "kinder, gentler Sid," he returned to his proven formula in all future weeks.

Oh, My!

During the long history of the *Sports Huddle,* no regular guest progressed as far as Twins manager Tom Kelly.

When he took over the reins from Ray Miller in 1986, Kelly was more than ready to manage a major league team, as he proved by winning a World Series in 1987 and again in 1991.

But as good as he was as a manager, he was bad as a radio personality. He had little time for ill-informed callers. He also had some classic arguments with Sid, including the time he lit into Sid for badmouthing his pitching coach, Dick Such.

Over time, Kelly became more comfortable with the show.

I always listened carefully for the cues that signaled the next few minutes were about to get interesting. One cue was whenever Tom responded to a caller with a sigh and the words, "Oh, my." Other times, I could just sense that he was ready to take on some persistent caller.

Even as Sid would be trying to dismiss the caller, I'd jump in with, "I think Tom wants to follow up on this one." I could just sense Kelly smiling in his Metrodome office.

"Now, what was the situation?" he would ask, nicely setting a trap from which there would be no escape.

"You had a runner on third and one out," the caller would remind him.

What followed was a baseball tutorial that was a thing of beauty.

"And who was my batter?"

"What kind of bunter is he?"

"Who was their pitcher?"

"What's his best pitch?"

"Where was the third baseman playing?"

"Who did I have left to pinch-hit?"

"What have they done against this guy?"

"Who was warming up in the bullpen?"

With Tom Kelly (right) at the fifteenth anniversary of the *Sports Huddle*
in 1996 on the Metrodome Plaza

"How do we hit that guy?"

He would drill deeper and deeper until the caller gave up in frustration.

It was Kelly's way of sharing what it was like to manage at the major league level, and nobody did it better.

Understanding Sid

Someone who knew I covered the Twins during the Billy Martin season once asked me if Billy was the most competitive person I had ever met. I said he was.

After working the past twenty-five years with Sid Hartman, I'd like to rephrase my answer. Sid is, without a doubt, the most tenacious competitor I've ever met. He simply hates to lose. And, like Billy, when he does lose, he takes it personally.

When there is breaking news, no one is more tenacious than Sid. He will call unlisted numbers, rouse people out of bed, pull them away from a dinner engagement, burst past a receptionist, or go through doors clearly marked "Do Not Disturb." He knows that relationships can be repaired, but deadlines can't wait.

I've seen him in action countless times. The technique may leave something to be desired, but the results can't be questioned. Here's one example.

When Mark McGwire, along with Sammy Sosa, was in hot pursuit of Roger Maris' single-season home-run record, the St. Louis Cardinals came to the Metrodome for interleague play.

As Sid and I met in the WCCO studios that morning a few minutes before the Tom Kelly Show, we talked about guests to get for later in the show.

"Why don't you get Mark McGwire," I joked. It was well known that McGwire was not taking interviews.

Missing the point of humor, Sid merely said, "Good idea."

Close to 10:30 a.m., Sid told our studio coordinator, Dave Schultz, to call the Metrodome, tell them it was Sid Hartman, and ask for the visitors' clubhouse.

"When you get the clubhouse attendant, don't tell him who it is. Just say that it's for McGwire and it's important."

"But, Sid," Schultz protested, "McGwire isn't talking to anyone."

"He'll talk to me," Sid said. "Just call there. Now."

So Schultz made the call, and thirty seconds later he whispered to me, "He's going to put McGwire on."

Moments later our listeners heard this exchange:

"Hello."

"Mark, this is Sid Hartman. How are you?"

"They told me this was an important personal call."

"Mark. It's Sid Hartman. We're on the radio right now."

"Sid, I'm not doing interviews. Any interviews."

"Mark, this will just take a minute. I really appreciate your coming on with us. We go back a long way—"

"Sid, I'm not—"

"Mark, talk about the pressure of chasing Maris."

"OK, you got me. Go ahead, but let's keep it short. I'm really not talking to anyone."

Many reporters would have given up at the point where McGwire said he wasn't doing interviews, but not Sid. He's heard and ignored that line so many times before.

People are always asking me what's going to happen to the *Sports Huddle* after Sid.

It's a fair question, but still quite premature. I have every reason to believe that Sid will continue to do the *Sports Huddle* for another ten years or more. He's still in great shape, and he enjoys doing what he does.

We should all be so lucky.

Sidisms

The main difference between Sid and someone like Yogi Berra is that Sid actually said all those lines that are attributed to him. A few years ago I started writing down some of the more memorable Sidisms. I only regret that I didn't start sooner.

When people ask me what my favorite Sidism is from the last twenty-five years of doing the *Sports Huddle* with him, I reply without hesitation: the interview with Tim Tschida.

This was during one of the years when controversy was brewing about the alleged differences in the strike zone between the American and National Leagues.

Tim Tschida, the St. Paul native who at one time was the American League's youngest umpire, was always a great interview. Both outspoken and articulate, Tschida was an ideal guest.

He also likes to talk, which isn't always a good thing for an interview with Sid, who prefers to do most of the talking.

On this occasion, Tschida was doing his usual good job of explaining something when Sid interrupted. Sid got right to the point.

"Isn't the real difference the umpires' lack of inconsistency?"

While Tim fumbled for an answer, I dove for a pen and a piece of paper.

"What was that?" Tschida said.

"The umpires. Their lack of inconsistency."

I had it. Word for word.

Upon getting to work on Monday, I sent a fax (this was before e-mail) to my former *Tribune* colleague Jerry Kirschenbaum, who was then an editor at *Sports Illustrated*. My phone rang a few minutes later.

"I love it," he said. "We're going to use it."

A week later I was ready. Magazine in hand, I said, "Sid, you made *Sports Illustrated* this week."

"I did?" he said. "Why?"

"Your interview with Tim Tschida."

"What does it say?"

"It quotes you, 'Isn't the real difference the umpires' lack of inconsistency?'"

"So?"

I've told that story every time we share a speaking platform. I think Sid still wonders why people laugh.

Dave Schultz, the *Sports Huddle* studio coordinator, is the person who selects the music that brings us back from each commercial break. Sid is oblivious to most of the music, but he always responds with a smile to a Frank Sinatra or a Dean Martin tune.

For the two to three weeks after he saw the musical *Mama Mia*, he responded well to various ABBA tunes, and once in a while he'll admit he likes Neil Diamond's "Sweet Caroline," even though he doesn't know who Diamond is.

During one show early in 2008, Schultz brought us back on the air with Gene Autry's "Back in the Saddle Again."

"Hey, Sid," I said. "That's your old friend Gene Autry."

"Yah?"

"You must have been pretty close to Autry back when he ran the Angels."

"I'm not trying to blow any smoke," said Sid, "but back in 1965 when the Twins went to the World Series for the first time, I was the president of the Baseball Writers Association. I had to get the guests for the winter banquet that year, and we had a lineup like they never had before. I got Carl Yastrzemski, and he was the American League MVP, and Orlando Cepeda, and he was the National League MVP."

"Both friends of yours from their Minneapolis Miller days, right?"

"Yes, sir."

"Who else did you get?"

"I was coming to that. I got Autry to fly in, and he was supposed to be on the program. But we never saw him. He was up in his hotel room having a few vibrations."

"Vibrations?"

Searching for the right word, Sid demonstrated by raising an invisible glass to his mouth.

"Libations?" I offered.

"If you say so."

Sid had fought hard to bring Major League Baseball and the National Football League to Minneapolis/St. Paul in the early 1960s. Before that, he campaigned for the building of Metropolitan Stadium as a future home for major league teams.

He was also an early and vocal advocate for the Metrodome. WCCO's Steve Cannon often accused Sid of having a personal and exclusive tunnel from the *Star Tribune* offices to the Metrodome, part of a deal struck to ensure his support.

When the Twins began expressing displeasure with the Metrodome as a baseball facility, Sid took note. He was convinced that the team would either leave the market or be contracted if a new ballpark wasn't built. He was frustrated that other cities were constructing new facilities for their teams while the Twins were having no success at the Minnesota State Legislature over a decade.

"I don't get it," Sid said on one of my favorite *Sports Huddle* shows. "Baltimore, Cleveland, Texas, Seattle, Cincinnati, Chicago, Pittsburgh, Philadelphia, Phoenix. They're building new ballparks everywhere in this country except here and Montreal."

When I later recounted that quote in front of an audience at a speaking engagement, Sid replied, "So what are you now—some kind of geography genius?"

Part of what comes across as Sid's shortness with callers results from his inability to clearly hear voices in certain tonal ranges. One of my favorite of Sid's exchanges with a caller illustrates this.

"Sid, our next caller is Gene from Chisago City."

"I don't like the way Gardy is handling his pitching staff—"

"How the hell do you know what Gardy is doing? You're from Chicago."

"Er, Sid, that would be Chisago City."

"Whatever. Next caller!"

As Barry Bonds approached Hank Aaron's home-run record, we took more and more calls on the *Sports Huddle* about the legitimacy of the record. Even though a majority of our callers thought the record would be tainted by Bonds' alleged use of performance-enhancing substances, Sid wasn't buying into it.

The week after Bonds broke the record, Sid decided it was time to tell it straight with a statement that left no room for doubt on where he stood.

"Don't you think he was tested for everything in the book? They tried and they tried and they came up with nothing. As far as I'm concerned, there is absolutely no proof that the guy ever used stereos."

"Steroids?" I suggested.

"Whatever!"

"And what about that Lipinski?" I said, in reference to the Olympic performance of U.S. figure skater Tara Lipinski the previous night.

Sid: "I don't care what people say he might have done. I still think the guy's been one hell of a president."

Sid, on changes in the University of Minnesota Athletic Department following a scandal: "Anyone in his right mind who didn't think there were going to be some changes is half crazy."

Stadium Squabbles

Over the years, Sid Hartman and I have disagreed on one topic far more than any other: the need for the University of Minnesota to have its own on-campus football stadium.

In the beginning, Sid argued that the Metrodome was a perfectly good home to Gopher football and that the university had made the right move when it abandoned an aging Memorial Stadium for downtown Minneapolis in 1982. He assured me and our WCCO radio listeners that there was "no chance" the Minnesota State Legislature would appropriate any money for a new stadium, and even if they did, he was convinced that the university would be unable to raise the additional money necessary to finish the construction.

I was a non-player in the decision to leave campus for the Metrodome. Like so many others, I was swept up in the glamour of the new domed facility and the argument that its presence would allow Minnesota to upgrade its recruiting by attracting better, faster high school athletes. Memorial Stadium was in decay, and why spend something like $10 million for repairs when the Metrodome was offering a fast track and free rent?

It was only after I started doing radio broadcasts of Gopher games that I began to see what was missing. In places like Madison (University of Wisconsin), Iowa City (University of Iowa), Columbus (the Ohio State University), Ann Arbor (University of Michigan), and

Happy Valley (Penn State University), huge numbers of students, faculty, and alumni come together on campus en masse for game days. That was no longer happening at the University of Minnesota. The Gopher athletic department had issued a mission statement that referred to Gopher sports as the "window" to the university, but in the case of football, that window looked into a house that was disconnected from the campus.

Former University of Minnesota president Mark Yudof, not much of a sports fan, quickly grasped the idea of returning football to campus. He talked often of fans parking in the ramp below Coffman Memorial Union and walking the mall for the first time in thirty years on their way to what was to become TCF Bank Stadium. He talked about the ways in which the university could reconnect with this generation of lost alumni.

The university created focus groups to explore the idea of bringing football back to campus. By far the most common memory recalled by people who were old enough to have experienced football on campus was that of the University of Minnesota Marching Band parading down University Avenue on a fall Saturday before turning and entering the stadium through the Memorial Arch.

That image, combined with the John Philip Sousa "Minnesota March" and the smell and sound of crunching autumn leaves, brought tears to the eyes of a number of those interviewed.

To Sid, that image translated into a traffic jam.

Two people who did a great deal to build a case for returning football to campus were athletic director Tom Moe and football coach Glen Mason. Long before it became a popular cause, the two of them used every platform they could find to make a case for an on-campus stadium.

As support for the stadium began to grow, Sid modified his position to campaign for a stadium on the Minnesota State Fair Grounds that would be large enough to accommodate both the Gophers and the Minnesota Vikings. That idea may have had some merit, but the State Fair Board quickly said that it had no interest in even exploring such a facility.

My arguments with Sid continued. Once he became convinced that an on-campus stadium had a chance with the legislature, he focused on the idea that 50,000 seats was far too few—even though he also contended that a new stadium would have no long-term impact on attendance.

The university's position was to build a 50,000-seat facility with the infrastructure in place to allow for expansion to 80,000. They wanted to create a demand for tickets, and the way to do that was to build in a degree of scarcity. In the sage words of my former business partner Dennis McGrath, "You don't build a church for Christmas and Easter."

Sid and I have agreed to disagree on the success of TCF Bank Stadium. We'll get a better feel for things when the Gophers open against the Air Force Academy on September 12, 2009. I plan to be there early to hear the band on University Avenue. We'll make sure Sid has a nice parking spot.

Sid continues to hold out hope of bringing the Vikings and Gophers together in the expanded TCF Bank Stadium. It's not going to happen.

His argument is that if no solution is found for the Vikings-stadium dilemma by the time the Metrodome lease expires in 2011, the Wilf family will sell the team to someone who will move it to another city that will gladly build a state-of-the-art facility to welcome an NFL team. I tend to agree with Sid on the point that the Wilfs would sell the team rather than break their promise to never move the team, but it was the Vikings who walked away from the idea of a joint facility on the University of Minnesota campus.

The Vikings have been vocal about their preference for building a new home on the Metrodome site in downtown Minneapolis. The price tag on a new Vikings stadium is approaching $1 billion, and in order to pay that tab, the team is going to need the participation of some government entity or public funding. The Vikings were unable to complete a proposed deal with Anoka County, and Hennepin County has little interest in pursuing a Vikings deal after the controversial partnership they made with the Minnesota Twins. The City of Minneapolis has a voter-imposed $10 million limit on any such project, and that wouldn't pay for the scoreboard in a new facility.

I believe there might be one governmental unit that could step forward to solve the Vikings' stadium situation. The Shakopee Mdewakanton tribe, which runs an impressive casino operation at Mystic Lake, has the space to accommodate a Vikings stadium. The casino is a first-class operation that has grown year after year. I would bet that the tribe would be happy to provide entertainment options for some 75,000 visitors on fall Sundays.

When I suggested this option to the Vikings, they said that it wouldn't work because part of the Wilf strategy has always been to do major development work in the vicinity of the stadium, and he wouldn't be able to do that on the tribal lands. I still think it's an option worth exploring.

The Mystic Lake solution would also leave the fully paid Metrodome in place. Although it may no longer be viable as a home for the Twins, Vikings, and Gophers, the Metrodome has served this community well, and I hope there is a way to keep it operating. The Sports Facilities Commission and executive director Bill Lester have done a great job of making the Metrodome available for everything from rollerblading to Super Bowls and Final Fours.

The Metrodome was built for a meager $55 million and has long since been paid off. With its major tenants about to depart, I'm convinced that its operators will be able to find a way to keep it filled more than 300 days per year.

WCCO, and a Modest Proposal for the Twins

It went almost unnoticed in June of 2007 when the Pohlad family purchased a local radio station in the Twin Cities. That same week I ran into Jim Pohlad and joked that he and his family should look into buying WCCO radio.

It was intended as a joke, but Jim clearly was interested.

"Is it for sale?" he asked.

"I'd be among the last to know," I said.

"Well, if CBS ever wanted to explore selling the station, I hope they would give us a call."

Now there's an interesting scenario. I hated the Twins' decision to leave WCCO for KSTP. I try to listen to every Twins game I can, and I can't get KSTP's signal in my office or my home.

I hope that some day the Pohlads might buy WCCO and return the Twins to that strong, familiar spot on the dial.

One weekend during the winter of 2007–08, Dave Lee offered to drive Sid Hartman and me to Fargo and introduce us to the audience at an agricultural expo at the Fargodome. Dave, WCCO's long-time morning voice, was still a legend there from his days on the morning show for KFGO.

We listened to WCCO all the way from downtown Minneapolis to downtown Fargo. The signal came through strong and clear the whole time.

We were riding in an SUV supplied by Walser Motors, one of

WCCO's major advertisers.

"Do you know why Walser advertises on WCCO Radio?" Dave asked.

"It's the only place they can get Dave Lee to endorse their products?" I volunteered.

"No. I'm serious," he said.

He had us stumped.

"They told me that they went to an ad agency who told them that our demographics were too old and that they could spend their money better elsewhere. So Walser decided to try an experiment. Every time a car came in for service, the technician turned on the radio to see what station their customers were listening to. By far the largest number of them were tuned to WCCO. That was good enough for Walser."

Whoever came up with that idea should get a promotion.

How About You?

It was clear from the first interview that Mark Dienhart was the best qualified candidate to be the number-two person for the University of Minnesota athletic department. I was on a search committee to find a capable candidate, and Dienhart had all the qualities we were looking for. He was smart, articulate, and interested.

He got the job, and during his years as senior associate athletic director and later as athletic director, he and I would talk on a number of subjects. I was delighted when he called one day in 1997 to say he thought he had a good chance to hire Glen Mason as the Gophers' new head football coach. We both felt the university needed an up-and-coming "name" coach to take over the job, and Mason was both available and ready to accept.

A year later, Mark called to ask if I had heard that Paul Flatley was stepping down from his decade-long job as football color commentator alongside Ray Christensen at WCCO Radio. Dienhart said his first choice for a replacement was to put a former Gopher football player alongside Ray. Mark knew that I had followed the program since I was sports editor of the *Minnesota Daily* in the 1960s, and he asked me to give him a list of potential analysts.

I came up with a half-dozen names, and Mark added a few more. The plan was to ascertain their levels of interest and let them work a few minutes alongside Ray in a mock game setting to see how they sounded.

About a month before the start of the season, Dienhart called again, while he was at a meeting of athletic directors in Florida.

"Do you by chance have any more names?" he asked.

I said I'd given him both my A and B lists and asked how things were coming.

"Not well," he confided. "We tried a number of guys with Ray, and it's just not working. We think one guy, Darrell Thompson, has real promise, but he's not ready to be a full-time analyst yet."

"Wow, the season's only a month away," I said.

"You're not telling me anything I don't know."

"Do you have any other ideas?" I asked.

"Just one. You."

"Mark, you've got to be kidding. You wanted a former Gopher football player. I never even played college football. You'd be setting yourself up for a lot of criticism."

"I've talked it over with Ray, and he likes the idea," he said. "I know you understand football, and nobody knows more about the history of Gopher football. If you'd be willing to do it, we'll also make an offer to Darrell. We'll go with a three-man crew. You interested?"

I didn't ask what it paid. I didn't ask about the length of the engagement. I didn't ask when I would start.

I just said yes.

Ray Christensen was a legend. He had been an integral part of my fall Saturdays for forty-seven years. I loved Ray's call of a game.

He tried his best to be impartial, but you knew where his loyalties were. I also enjoyed his sense of humor and his occasional use of a pun, often followed by an apology.

I remembered a game, maybe fifteen or twenty years earlier, when Ray read a commercial for Midwest Federal, then came out of the spot to join the band in a stirring version of the William Tell Overture, which was also the theme song for the *Lone Ranger* TV series.

He couldn't resist sharing with listeners: "So, we go from a loan arranger to the Lone Ranger."

Minutes before he and I signed on for our first game together, I reminded him of that line.

"A terrible pun," he recalled, smiling broadly.

I worked with Ray for three years. He said he thought that fifty years in the football booth was a nice number. As we traveled around the Big Ten, I was always impressed with how highly regarded Ray was at visiting schools. His legend carried far beyond Minnesota. During his fiftieth season, Ray was honored or recognized at every school we visited.

In response to the frequently asked question of how I was chosen to work with Ray, the consummate gentleman, I often told people, "Getting to work three years with Ray was my reward for working fifteen years with Sid."

When Ray finally decided it was time to hang it up, Dave Lee was the logical person to succeed him at the play-by-play job. An excellent athlete from Hatton, North Dakota, Lee did play-by-play broadcasts in Fargo before joining WCCO as a key part of its morning drive team. WCCO quickly promoted its post-Christensen team as "Gopher football in 3D, with Dave, Darrell, and Dave." Mike Grimm joined the broadcasts in 2007 to provide assistance on pregame, halftime, and postgame shows. All of us are united in the pursuit of one goal: to one day do a postseason game from Pasadena.

With former Gophers football great Darrell Thompson and Dave Lee
in the radio booth for a Gophers game at Colorado State University

A Super Effort

The call from the governor's office was brief and to the point. Governor Rudy Perpich had cleared time on his schedule and was expecting to see us at 2 p.m. that day. Coming at 10 a.m., it sounded more like a command than an invitation.

I showed up in the Governor's waiting room at 1:50. Once I saw who else was there, the topic of the meeting was no longer in doubt.

What we had was pretty much Minnesota's losing Super Bowl team. We had been turned down twice by the National Football League in our efforts to host the game, and no one had much of a stomach to try a third time.

Already in the office were Marilyn Nelson, future head of the Carlson Company; Harvey Mackay, fresh from the success of his first book; Mike Lynn, the general manager and soon-to-be president of the Minnesota Vikings; Bill Lester, who had taken over from Jerry Bell as the top man at the Metrodome; Paul Ridgeway, whose fame for special events planning was already well known; and me, the head of the Mona Meyer McGrath & Gavin public relations firm.

Governor Perpich got right to the point.

"What's this talk I hear about not going for another Super Bowl? They're already calling me Governor Goofy. But I really think we can do this. We didn't come that close just to pack our bags and go home."

Why was he hearing this negative talk, he wondered aloud.

"Governor," Mike Lynn explained, "we can get all the promises we want out of these owners, but when they go behind closed doors they'll always vote with their swimming suits and golf clubs."

"I'm sure you're right, Mike," Perpich said, "but there must be something we can do to level the playing field."

Lynn said there was one chance, and that was to convince the NFL owners to award a Super Bowl to a northern city some time in the future. The event had been outside of the South only once, and most people considered that event, in Detroit in 1982, to be perhaps the worst Super Bowl in history.

Marilyn and Harvey were quick to follow Lynn's reasoning.

"I think Mike's right," Marilyn said. "We'll never beat New Orleans and Miami in head-to-head competition, but we've got a good chance against any other northern city."

Mackay was already into strategies. "We're going straight after the owners this time. This is going to be just like a political election, and we've got to get a majority of twenty-eight votes."

Perpich smiled, knowing that the conversation was no longer about whether to mount another assault on the NFL owners, but how to do it. In classic DFL fashion, he offered to double our budget from the zero state dollars we had received the first time around.

Word quickly spread that we were going to make another try at a Super Bowl. Members of the media, led by Sid Hartman, were of a single mind.

"Look," Sid said to me, "I'm telling you as a friend, you have no chance of getting a Super Bowl to come here. Zero. None. I have all the respect in the world for Marilyn Nelson and Harvey, but the owners just don't want to come here, and you are wasting your time."

What greater motivation did we need?

We met the next week in Marilyn's office at the Carlson Center. Mike Lynn had given some further thought to his plan.

"There's an owners meeting coming up," he said. "Not a real heavy agenda, and we aren't going to be awarding any Super Bowls. I'm going to call some of the owners of northern teams. We'll make the point that the league was founded in the North and that more than half of our teams are in the northern half of the country. A lot of these cities are either building new stadiums or talking about building new stadiums. It'll be a tremendous boost to those guys if we can say that some day they might host a Super Bowl. They don't have to pick any specific city. They just need to vote to have a Super Bowl up north in about four or five years. It just might work."

Marilyn suggested that we needed to know a lot more about the owners.

"Let's find out where they went to college," said Harvey. "Where do their kids go to school? What Minnesotans sit on their boards?

Who are their customers? Their suppliers? Their neighbors? We need to start making visits and phone calls. We need them to be contacted by people they know and trust."

Slowly we began to build extensive files on each owner and to cross-check them against people we knew and trusted. Mackay was incredible at this. He would have made a great detective.

The previous times we had pursued the Super Bowl, we had made a case for why America should come to Minnesota on the last weekend in January. Each time, we received warm praise from the owners for our style and perseverance, but we didn't get their votes. This time it was all about their votes.

First, Mike needed to get the vote to go north at some time in the future.

Trading votes on other issues and working the phones constantly with the other northern teams, he was able to prevail.

No sooner had that happened when both Phoenix and San Francisco tried to have themselves declared northern cities. Their efforts failed, but not without some heated discussion.

It was now inevitable that the league's prize possession was coming north, and we needed to be ready with our bid.

The league invited all the bidding cities to an owners meeting in Los Angeles. Each city was given a thick bidding document and urged to come to the meeting with any questions. Jim Steeg, the league official in charge of special events such as the Super Bowl, presided at the meeting.

Most cities were reluctant to ask questions that would give away any of their strategies, but there were a number of common concerns.

In a meeting that lasted more than four hours—interrupted only by a surprise news conference to announce Commissioner Pete Rozelle's resignation—we went through the bid book section by section. It was a complicated process that begged for interpretation.

"On page 160, paragraph three, it says, 'the League will entertain a sharing of revenues from the game-day sale of Super Bowl merchandise at the host venue'," a representative from Indianapolis read. "Can the league give us any indication what it means when it says a 'sharing of revenues'?"

A weary Steeg, approaching the meeting's three-hour mark, looked up from the page and explained. "I'll be honest with you on that one, guys. We want it all."

Finally, a direction we could understand.

Although the National Football League is often depicted as greedy, the league representatives were more than reasonable throughout these discussions.

Several cities offered things that were little more than neatly packaged bribes. Time and again, Steeg said no.

"Be yourself," he'd say. "Don't pretend it's not going to be cold. We're already past that decision."

Armed with that advice, we decided to test his sense of humor. One of the lines in the questionnaire asked for the "mean temperature" of Super Bowl weekend in your community.

Bill Lester and his staff were in charge of filling out the technical aspects of the bid; I dealt with the community issues.

Shortly before submitting the bid, we met with our entire committee to have them look over what we were proposing.

After "Mean Temperature" I had written, "Yes," and left it at that.

Four cities were vying to be named host of Super Bowl XXVI in 1992: Detroit, Seattle, Indianapolis, and Minneapolis. Among the four candidates, we had the coldest climate, and everyone knew it. After a short debate, we submitted it the way I wrote it.

"That one made me laugh," Steeg later told us, "and I don't laugh a lot during the week of Super Bowl selections."

Representatives from the four competing cities were invited to New Orleans to give their presentations in May of 1989. Working with Russell Manning Studios in Minneapolis, we put together a tight twenty-minute presentation. Harvey, the master salesman, made the pitch. Marilyn, an excellent and persuasive presenter, handled the close. We had drawn the straw to present first, and we had, by far, the most complicated visual needs, with twelve projectors to be coordinated. Because we were going first, we offered to have our audiovisual team handle AV needs throughout the morning to save the NFL the expense and time of setting up four different equipment packages. The NFL was quick to accept our offer.

Four different sources—*USA Today,* the *New Orleans Times Picayune,* and two insider newsletters—were at our doors in the hotel the morning of the presentations. There was a great deal of interest in this selection process, and each publication predicted the finish. Seattle, Indianapolis, and Detroit each got first-place votes. The only thing on which they all agreed was that Minneapolis would be the first city eliminated.

Sid Hartman, on his 6:40 a.m. show on WCCO Radio, assured his listeners that he loved Marilyn, Harvey, Mona, and the others to death, but we had "no chance" of getting the Super Bowl.

At breakfast that morning Lynn was upbeat. "How's everyone feeling? You have a good night's sleep? This is going to be fun.

"Here's the deal," he said. "We need to get it down to us and Detroit. If that happens, we're in."

We all went over the likely first-round votes. Many of the owners had told us how they intended to vote, and it was clear that no city had enough support to win on the first vote.

"We'll take a couple of votes, and nobody's going to win," Lynn said. "Then someone will look at the clock and suggest that the low vote-getter gets dropped. That'll pass. We'll drop two cities in the next two votes. You can cross your fingers that it's between us and Detroit at that point."

As it turned out, Lynn hit the nail right on the head. After several rounds of voting in which no city received a majority, the committee would decide to eliminate the low vote-getter in each round. Because Indianapolis and Seattle were newer members of the league, Lynn knew that they would have less support compared to the more established NFL cities of Minneapolis and Detroit.

As the meetings began, about 250 reporters and representatives of the four competing cities huddled in small groups outside the meeting room. Each of the cities filled the allotted twenty minutes for presentations. After a short break, the deliberations began.

What only we knew was that our communications team from Russell Manning was sitting in the projection room, listening to the discussions. One by one throughout the meeting, they left to take bathroom breaks.

"They're deadlocked and going to start dropping one city at a time," we learned.

About fifteen minutes later, we heard, "Indianapolis is out."

Twenty minutes later it was, "Seattle's out."

No one on our team made eye contact with anyone else. It was now down to the situation that Mike Lynn had described.

Each of the two remaining cities had a final chance to state its case. Detroit's owners said that they would add additional police the weekend of the event to ensure the security of attendees. They reminded owners that the auto companies were major advertisers who would look kindly upon the choice of Detroit.

Lynn—who knew that the best form of public relations is what others say about you, not what you say about yourself—let competing owners speak for Minnesota.

It had been prearranged that Miami owner Joe Robbie was to rise on our behalf at that point, but Robbie had been hospitalized with a medical emergency that morning. His son, Tim, did a great job for Minnesota, but he didn't carry the clout or connections of his father.

Next, Jim Finks asked to speak. Finks was with the New Orleans Saints at the time, but he had been the general manager of the Minnesota Vikings from 1964 to 1973. Finks' family was raised in Edina, and he was an unapologetic booster for Minneapolis and St. Paul. He also was one of the most respected voices at league meetings and had been mentioned as a possible successor to Rozelle. Finks and Lynn had talked beforehand about what he was going to say if things got to this point.

Finks began with comments about how well the people in Minnesota would handle the event, and then he played his trump card.

"Gentlemen," he said, "these are two great cities. In that regard you can't make a bad choice, but let me give you something to think about. Only once before has the Super Bowl ever been held in the North and that was in Detroit.

"We are going all over the country urging cities to join with their local ownerships in building new, state-of-the-art stadiums. When we do that, we look them in the eye and tell them that if they will build those stadiums, that we some day will bring the Super Bowl, our prized possession, to their communities. It's the Super Bowl that helps generate the economic impact to justify those investments. If we vote today to send the Super Bowl back to Detroit, we are saying that in the future there will be southern Super Bowls and Detroit Super Bowls, and I don't need to tell you what that means for your plans for new stadiums."

Three minutes after Finks sat down, the door to the audiovisual room opened. "We're in" was muttered en route to the bathroom.

Seconds later the doors to the ballroom opened and a league representative told the media they were to gather in a nearby conference room for an important announcement in about ten minutes.

Already knowing the outcome, we took positions along the far wall. Incoming commissioner Paul Tagliabue was going to make the announcement. We could hear the speculation among the reporters.

"It's Detroit," one said confidently. "I heard it last night." A Seattle station prepared to go live. The reporter had former Viking running back Hugh McElhenny, a member of their delegation, wired for reaction.

Tagliabue milked it well, saying nice things about each finalist and talking about how difficult it had been to make a decision. However, he said, "I'm pleased to announce that the 1992 Super

Bowl will be played in [long dramatic pause] the Metrodome in Minneapolis, Minnesota."

The announcement was greeted with shock by all those who had believed their morning newspapers. "No way," people said out loud. "How could they?" another asked.

Marilyn Nelson and Harvey Mackay lined up to do a series of interviews with the astonished Minnesota television reporters who had made the long trip down the Mississippi.

Somewhere in Minneapolis, Sid began making a case for knowing it all along.

Mike the Big Tipper

Mike Lynn, who was majority owner of the Minnesota Vikings at the time, deserves a lot of the credit for bringing the Super Bowl to Minnesota. Although much of his work took place out of the spotlight, he was the architect behind what actually went on during the voting process. He also was part of a humorous episode that happened on one occasion when Minnesota tried for and did not get the Super Bowl.

Representatives from the Twin Cities were invited to an owners meeting in Washington, D.C. The rumor was that the owners might name as many as four host cities for future games, and our chances had never looked better.

The selection committee convened in a Washington hotel in the middle of the morning. We, along with representatives of a dozen other competing cities, were told to be ready to give our presentation when we were called.

Our team included Governor Rudy Perpich, Senator Rudy Boschwitz, best-selling author Harvey Mackay, business leader Marilyn Nelson, and other civic leaders. The presentations took most of the morning and much of the afternoon. We were told not to go far from the ballroom in case the owners had questions. We stayed outside the closed doors while lunch was served. We stayed there as a catered dinner arrived and was taken away. We stayed there until 10:15 p.m., when Commissioner Pete Rozelle announced the four cities that would host future Super Bowls. We were not one of them.

Lynn was astounded to find that we had taken turns getting food from vending machines while the league kept us waiting for more than twelve hours.

"Come on," he told all of us. "I'm buying dinner. It's the least I can do."

We took cabs to a French restaurant, where we consumed wonderful food and wine until sometime after two o'clock in the morning when we took cabs back to our hotel as a light rain fell.

It was a nice ending to a bad day, and the good feeling remained for more than a decade, when I once again crossed paths with Marvelous Mike Lynn.

"Do you remember that time in Washington when the NFL kept you guys outside a hotel room for something like twelve hours?" he asked.

"I remember it. It was fourteen hours," I countered.

Ignoring the correction, Mike was rolling.

"Do you remember that we all went out to a French restaurant? Do you remember that when we were waiting for a cab in the rain that the maitre d' came out looking for me?"

That I did not recall.

"Well, he did. He kept saying, 'Monsieur Lynn, Monsieur Lynn.' I was probably talking to somebody and didn't hear him, but he finally found me and asked if he could have a word with me.

197

"'Ze food? Ze food was all right?' he said.

"'Yah, the food was great,' I told him.

"'And the wine was up to your expectations?'

"'The wine was terrific.'

"'Ze service? Perhaps ze service was not up to par?'

"Now, I may not be the brightest guy, but I assumed he wasn't happy with my tip. I told him that everything was just great, but if he didn't think I'd left a big enough tip that I'd be willing to make an adjustment. We went back inside and I told him that the bill was something like $195 and I left a tip of $50.

"'Perhaps Monsieur Lynn would like to see ze bill one more time,' he said.

"I took a good look at it and it was for $1,950, and I'd left a tip for $50. The last of the big tippers."

Fantasy Camp

Whoever coined the phrase "anything that doesn't kill you makes you stronger" must have written it after attending a major league baseball fantasy camp.

I went to the Twins Fantasy Camp for three straight years in the mid 1990s.

Like most campers, I began serious training in preparation for camp about a week before leaving frozen Minnesota for a week at the Twins training facility near Fort Myers, Florida, in January. The hardest part of the preparation was finding my decades-old glove, which was approximately as flexible as its owner.

While preparing for my second visit to Fantasy Camp, I must have said something to longtime friend Bill Popp, and he decided to join me. I may have left out the parts about the pain and suffering.

To get in a little practice work before the trip down south, Bill and I headed for an indoor batting cage. The machines we stepped into had been set at slow-pitch softball speed. It seemed that hitting a baseball wasn't nearly as tough as major leaguers would have you believe.

After about a dozen shots into the netting, we were interrupted by the facility manager.

"Getting ready for an old-timers softball tourney?" he offered.

"Softball! We're going to Twins Fantasy Camp next week."

"Then you might want to adjust the speed a little bit," he suggested. "What speed do you want?"

Knowing that Nolan Ryan could approach a hundred miles per hour on a radar gun, and knowing that Nolan Ryan was not going to be anywhere near Fort Myers, I suggested seventy-five miles per hour.

The manager smiled and stuck around to watch the action.

Make that inaction.

I swung at and missed fifteen straight missiles. Popp managed two foul balls and what might have passed for a groundout to the pitcher.

At sixty miles an hour we were able to make more than occasional contact, and at fifty miles an hour we were nearing our zone.

Hands aching but batting eyes properly honed, we went home to pack for the week.

The entry fee of $3,500 included a uniform, cap, and socks. The last thing I added to my bag was a full bottle of Advil, which turned out to be the best decision I made all week.

Most of the sixty campers arrived in Fort Meyers on Saturday. We all stayed at the same motel, and Saturday night was the kickoff banquet, which featured among the attendees Harmon Killebrew, Tony Oliva, Mudcat Grant, Bert Blyleven, Rich Rollins, Frank Quilici, Earl Battey, Julio Becquer, John Castino, Gene Larkin, and about a dozen other former players.

After dinner, Blyleven and Grant introduced the first-timers to Kangaroo Court. All the money collected during the week would be contributed to the Twins Community Fund.

The rules were simple. Blyleven and Grant would take notes during the day and dispense fines at night. Not running out a ground ball or failing to back up a throw would cost you three dollars. Swearing at an umpire would cost you five dollars. Failure to swear at an umpire could also cost you five dollars. You were encouraged to appeal any decision you did not agree with. An appeal cost you five dollars. Failing to have your appeal upheld cost you five dollars. In the three years I attended Twins Fantasy Camp, not a single appeal was upheld.

With Harmon Killebrew at Twins Fantasy Camp in 1994

To get things started the first night, Blyleven fined me five dollars for knowing Sid Hartman. I thought I got off easy.

On Sunday we were randomly assigned to teams. We played a doubleheader of two five-inning games while the coaches watched and evaluated talent for the upcoming draft.

It was surprising how well we played that first day. Legs that hadn't been stretched in twenty years did not yet ache, and arms that hadn't been asked to propel a baseball in decades responded with their last bit of muscle memory.

The trouble began when the alarm went off at 6:45 Monday morning. Joints that felt fine at 10 p.m. refused to respond eight hours later. And that was just the beginning.

As the week wore on, the pains kept pace. We played doubleheaders on Monday and Tuesday. There was a single game Wednesday morning. Thursday was a doubleheader against the Red Sox campers who came to Fort Meyers. On Friday we took buses to Sarasota to play the White Sox campers. Saturday was the big game against the former Twins. Not counting Sunday's opening-day pickup game, that was a total of ten games in six days. Most of the campers hadn't played ten games in twenty years.

I began to take Advils like they were M&Ms. It was the only way to keep going.

Bill Popp's wife, Teri, found a massage therapist three blocks from our motel. She made an appointment for Bill after one of the doubleheaders. The therapist worked on his legs for an hour, trying to unwind the knots. She kept him for a second hour and drove him back to the hotel, fearing that he would not be able to cover the three blocks before darkness fell.

Earl Battey, the former all-star catcher, was the manager of my team. I was playing second base and batting seventh in the first game against the White Sox in Sarasota.

The average age of our team was fifty-two. The White Sox players, in general, were older. Their third baseman brought a cup of beer into the field with him each inning and carefully removed it any time an opposing runner approached. Their second baseman smoked a cigar throughout the game.

I knew we were in trouble as soon as their pitcher began to warm up. The sound got to us first. Pop Pop Pop—the sound of a fastball hitting the catcher's glove.

The pitcher was thirty years old and had been the ace of his college staff seven years earlier. Fantasy Camp was an anniversary present from his Barbie Doll wife and, in his mind, the route to the majors.

His fastball, once clocked in the low nineties according to his teammates, now barely reached the low eighties. It looked and sounded like the batting cage gun on steroids.

He struck out the side in the first inning, and then walked one batter in the second, bringing me to the plate with one on and two out. Hoping to catch a base on balls, I crowded the plate.

Huge mistake.

His first pitch came inside and I tried to duck out of the way. It hit me just above the left elbow. Despite the continuous application of ice packs, the arm swelled and turned a solid purple color from my watchband up to my shoulder.

Ready to take my cuts at the plate

Knowing that a doubleheader was scheduled for the next day, I decided to sit out the second game against the White Sox, sharing base-coaching duties with Battey.

Tom Paciorek, a former major league outfielder, was pitching for the White Sox in the second game and doing a good job of lobbing pitches over the heart of the plate. We were down there to have fun, which he clearly understood. Our batters were making solid contact, but ninety feet to first base was a long way for guys with turned ankles and swollen hamstrings.

Cupping a cigarette in his fingers and leaning against the dugout rail, Battey laughed quietly as we tried to launch a rally.

"What's so funny?" I asked him.

"I shouldn't tell you," he said.

"Come on."

"OK, but I don't mean for anyone to take this the wrong way. Looking at you guys playing today reminds me of the Special Olympics."

I winced as he made his point, but there were several moments when it was hard to disagree with him.

One of our players made solid contact and rifled a one-hop shot off the left-field fence. It may have been the hardest hit ball of the week (with the exception of a left-field home run by Twins broadcaster Dick Bremer). The left fielder played the ball nicely off the fence and made an on-target throw to the short fielder, who wheeled and one-hopped the ball to the shortstop, who turned and decided against throwing to first—because the runner was already three-fourths of the way there.

The only doubles came on fielding misplays, and triples were out of the question.

The highlight of the week was the Saturday game against the former Twins, which was played at Lee County Stadium. My wife, Linda, sang the national anthem.

In the previous year's game, I had singled past third base off Rich Rollins. This year I was facing Blyleven, and I didn't like the look on his face. All week he had worked with campers on how to throw a curve ball. He failed to offer any advice on how to hit one, however.

Looking from the other side, it suddenly looked a lot more lethal.

I swung and missed on strike one and fouled the second pitch into the dirt. Bert was grinning broadly. "Curve ball," he yelled as he went into his windup.

Remembering the inside pitch from the White Sox hurler the day before, I hit the ground at home plate as Blyleven's perfect curve ball made its way from behind me to a spot over the inside corner of the plate.

"Strike three," the umpire barked.

"I balked," Blyleven hollered. "Get your ass back in there, and this time don't duck."

This time I swung and missed, becoming in my mind the 3,702nd strikeout victim of what should have been a Hall of Fame career.

The idea of Fantasy Camp was to let the campers fulfill their baseball fantasy. That meant if you wanted to pitch, you got to pitch.

Barry Karon was a cardiologist at the Mayo Clinic. He was a large person. In today's terms, his role model would have been Cleveland pitcher C. C. Sabathia.

Barry had a gravity-defying, 29-mile-per-hour fastball. It didn't register on the radar gun, but Blyleven said he clocked it with his calendar.

Gene Larkin, the game-seven hero of the 1991 World Series, stepped up to the plate against the crafty cardiologist.

Barry's first pitch was halfway on its journey to bouncing in front of the plate when Larkin started his swing. He had time to resume his stance and swing again if he had thought to, but he was laughing too hard.

"Strike one," the umpire growled.

Our dugout was respectfully quiet. Larkin's teammates began to get on him. I thought I heard Quilici's or Boswell's voice, but at Kangaroo Court that night they all pleaded innocent to charges of harassing a teammate.

Larkin dug in, determined to wait out the next pitch. His second effort produced a harmless foul ball in the home-plate dirt. Strike two.

The pressure was on and Larkin began to sweat. He was one pitch away from undoing his World Series heroics. Nervously, Karon toed the pitching rubber, pondering which of his one-pitch repertoire to use.

Larkin, knowing he wasn't patient enough to wait for the pitch to reach home plate, waited for the windup and quickly moved ten feet in front of the plate. He lined a one-hopper off the fence in right. Still able to run and having a ten-foot advantage, he easily turned it into a triple.

At the closing banquet that night, each of the players was asked to speak. Some told old stories of their days with the Twins. Others talked about how they got into baseball and what they were doing now.

Larkin was the last to speak. Everyone in the room expected him to talk about his game-winning Series hit.

It was clear that he had thought about what he was going to say, but none of the aching campers was prepared for what followed.

"I found something here this week," Larkin said, "and I need to thank you guys for it. I really didn't have any idea what to expect. I'd heard about Fantasy Camp, but I thought it was just a bunch of old guys playing catch. And then I got here and saw that I had a locker between Tony Oliva and Earl Battey. And we talked baseball every day.

"I saw a guy tear up both hamstrings as bad as anything I've ever seen. He could barely get in and out of the whirlpool tub at night, and he couldn't walk to his car without someone helping him. Injuries that bad would have kept my teammates on the disabled list for a month. But this guy came out the next day and caught both ends of a doubleheader.

"I saw one of the ladies take a pop fly on the forehead, which knocked her out. And she was back in the lineup three innings later.

"I heard people talk about baseball and how much they loved the game. For one week there was nobody complaining about their salary. Hey, you guys paid money to be here. Nobody complained about anything.

"So, I want to thank my teammates and I want to thank you guys and ladies. You reminded me how much I love this game, and I'm grateful for it."

No one had expected it. Larkin was not the only person with tears in his eyes.

Blyleven fined him five dollars.

"General principles," he said. "There's no crying in baseball."

Golf Club Wisdom

Over the years I've had a chance to play in dozens, if not hundreds, of charity golf events. One of my favorites, which took place in the late 1990s, put me in a group with former Minnesota Viking Bob Lurtsema, sportscaster Mark Rosen, and Bud Chapman.

The star of that group was Chapman, who in his late sixties was the state's seniors champion at the time.

Although Bud is an outstanding golfer, he is far better known as an artist. His paintings of the "18 Infamous Golf Holes" hang in thousands of country clubs and golf shops around the world. His locales include the Grand Canyon, the Smoky Mountains, the Alps, Okefenokee Swamp, and Big Sur. The 85-yard, par 2, 17th is played high above Wall Street, and the 18th is an amazing par 6,947-yard challenge along the slippery face of Iguassu Falls in Brazil.

Our immediate challenge was Rolling Green Golf Club in Medina, a relatively easy course for someone with the skills and imagination of Chapman.

Bud also was by far the slightest in stature in our group. Using an overly long driver that came nearly to his chest, he routinely placed his drives anywhere from 30 to 45 yards beyond our best.

Hole after hole we would crush our drives, only to pick them up in favor of Bud's (as are the rules in a scramble). In a case of our massive swings versus his perfect timing, it was simply no contest.

Finally, Rosen said what was on all of our minds.

"Bud," he said, "I don't want this to come out wrong, but all of us are wondering how a guy your age can hit a golf ball so far."

"I'm not offended," Bud said. "I get that question a lot. And every time I do, I think about something Lee Travino once told me.

"'Bud,' he said, 'the golf clubs have no idea whatsoever how old you are.'"

With full credit to Bud and Lee, I've used that anecdote in hundreds of speeches to illustrate that all too often we work under self-imposed restraints.

The Wizard of Westwood

You never know when a business lunch will turn out to be one you'll never forget.

In the early 1990s, David Weiner, a friend and occasional client, said he was bringing a friend to town and was setting up a lunch with some business associates in a private room at Sofitel, in Edina. The identity of the special guest was a secret, but we knew of Weiner's friendship with Sandy Koufax, so that was the early speculation.

Weiner greeted us at the front desk and led us to a small room at the rear of the restaurant. A scholarly man was sitting alone at the table autographing a small stack of books.

"Gentlemen," Weiner said, "I'd like you to meet a friend of mine."

John Wooden needed no further introduction. He was the most recognized legend in college basketball history, and he was all ours for the next two hours.

Wooden shook his head and smiled. "I'm not sure I'm capable of filling the next two hours with conversation," he said. "But we'll just talk for a while and see how it goes."

Wooden was the first person ever inducted into the Basketball Hall of Fame as both a player and a coach. He is widely regarded as the best coach in the history of college basketball, and his ten NCAA championships at UCLA is a record that has never been approached.

As a high school player, Wooden led his Martinsville, Indiana, team to the state championship finals for three straight years, winning the title in 1927. He was an All-State selection all three years. When he was at Purdue University, he was named three times to the All-America team. The 1932 team was named national champions by the Helms Athletic Foundation. (The NCAA did not hold an official championship competition until 1939.)

Wooden graduated from Purdue in 1932 with a degree in English and later earned a master's degree from Indiana State Teacher's College (later Indiana State University).

After college he spent several years playing professionally while also teaching and coaching high school. His biography says he once made 134 consecutive free throws as a pro, and he was named to the first team of the fledgling National Basketball League. When World War II broke out, he enlisted in the navy, where he served as a lieutenant.

After the war he returned to Indiana and was hired as the coach at Indiana State. In 1947 his team won a conference title and received an invitation to play in the National Association of Intercollegiate Basketball (NAIB) National Tournament in Kansas City. Wooden refused the invitation because of an NAIB policy banning African American players. Wooden's team featured Clarence Walker, an African American from East Chicago, Indiana. The next year the NAIB changed its rules. That year Wooden's Indiana State team made it to the finals but lost to Louisville. Walker became the first African

American to play in a postseason basketball tournament. After that tournament, things got interesting for this legendary coach.

At our lunch, Wooden said that all questions were fair game, and I went first.

"I have a close personal friend named Sid Hartman," I said, "and he maintains that both you and Bobby Knight would have been head basketball coaches at the University of Minnesota if Minnesota hadn't screwed things up. Is that story true?"

Wooden smiled and sat back. "I would never presume to speak for Mr. Knight, so you'll have to ask him that one some other time. But in my case, the Minnesota story is very much the truth."

He had our complete attention as he closed his eyes momentarily, sighed slightly, and started to tell the story.

My wife, Nellie, and I always talked everything over. We loved the Midwest and very much wanted to stay in this part of the country. I thought there was a high level of high school basketball being played in Indiana and the rest of the region.

Our success at Indiana State was starting to draw attention, and I was contacted about the head coaching job at Minnesota. It was an attractive job that seemed to offer all that we were looking for, and I was ready to accept the job.

They said they wanted to hire me, but they wanted me to keep Dave McMillen [the incumbent coach] as an assistant. I didn't think that was fair to either one of us, and I told them as much.

They said they needed a little time to work things out, and I was honest with them that I was also talking with UCLA and that they had a deadline by which I had to tell them either yes or no.

We had it arranged with Minnesota that they would call me an hour before I had to tell UCLA what I was going to do.

Well, we waited for that call and it just didn't come. So I told UCLA that I would accept their offer. Almost exactly an hour later the call came through from Minnesota. They said that a big snowstorm had knocked the wires down and they couldn't get a phone call through to me. They said they had everything worked out.

I had to tell them that, when I didn't hear from them, I accepted the job at UCLA. We all felt just terrible about it, but I was a man of my word, and I couldn't even consider going back on my decision.

Wooden took over at UCLA in 1948 and coached there until he retired in 1975. During those years his Bruins won ten national championships (1964, 1965, 1967, 1968, 1969, 1970, 1971, 1972, 1973, and 1975). The team won eighty-eight straight games between January 1971 and January 1974; no team has come within forty-two games of that streak since. He left UCLA with a record of 620 wins and just 147 losses. During that same span, under coaches Ozzie Cowles, John Kundla, Bill Fitch, George Hanson, Bill Musselman, and Jim Dutcher, Gopher teams won 362 and lost 266.

Men who played Vikings football under Bud Grant delight in telling about their introduction to their new head coach. Whereas they were expecting to learn the basics of a new offense and defense, Bud demonstrated the proper technique for lining up during the playing of the "Star Spangled Banner."

Hall of Famer Bill Walton talks about learning from Wooden the proper way to put on socks. Was that truth or legend?

"Oh, heavens," Wooden chuckled. "People like to make so much out of that, but I suppose it was true. Wrinkles can lead to blisters, and blisters can take you off the floor. And besides, it's such a little thing that once you learn to do it right, you don't ever need to learn it again."

He could have been talking about putting on socks or executing a successful pick and roll. The principles are the same.

Then there was the time when he was confronted by the changing trends in personal style. The crewcuts and clean-shaven look of the 1950s and early 1960s were giving way to the grunge of the

Vietnam-era late 1960s. Could the conservative Wooden impose his will on free spirits such as center Bill Walton?

Again, the chuckle. "Oh, I've told this story so many times I think people must be sick of hearing it.

"Long hair and facial hair were showing up all over campus at that time and there was a lot of speculation as to what my reaction would be. There was a lot of talk on campuses all over the United States about student rights, and we weren't exempt.

"We always had a little team meeting before the first day of practice, and I wanted the boys to know exactly how I felt. So, I was honest with them. I always tried to be honest with them. I told them that I had been talked to by the administration and they told me that we were entering a new era in relationships with our students. They pointed out to me that how students wear their hair and whether or not they have facial hair were strictly their individual rights and that I have no authority to tell anybody that they should cut their hair or shave their beards. And I agreed with them. So, I wasn't going to do that, I assured them.

"What I do have control over is who plays and who sits on the bench."

The next day every player arrived looking just like all Wooden teams looked in the past.

"The amount of playing time can be a great motivator," he observed.

It was becoming clear during the course of our lunch that in addition to all his other well-known qualities, Wooden had a keen sense of humor, which he was about to demonstrate in one final anecdote.

We asked him how closely he still followed basketball, and he said that he tried to get to all the UCLA home games but wasn't traveling much anymore.

Once again the smile flashed, and he was off in a new direction.

"They did try to get me back to Indiana not long ago. Tried really hard," he said.

"A number of years ago they picked an all-time Indiana basketball team, and I was fortunate enough to be named one of the guards, along with Oscar Robertson.

"The people on that committee have been so good to me over the years, and they'd never do anything to hurt my feelings. Well, they started calling me and sending me things. Turns out there was this wonderful player for Bedford North Lawrence named Damon Bailey. [Bailey scored 3,134 points and was the state's all-time leading scorer at the high school level.]

"They kept telling me about Bailey, and they wanted me to come back and see him. I asked them why it was so important for me to see him, and they reluctantly said that some of them were talking about revising the All-Time Indiana High School team to make room for Bailey.

"'But we won't do it unless you tell us it's all right,' they said.

"So I told them flat out that I didn't think it was a very good idea.

"'Why not?' they asked.

"'Because,' I told them, 'I don't think Oscar is going to like it.'"

From the Bench

When major figures in the world of sports visit Minneapolis/St. Paul, it's a good bet that they will be asked to speak to the Twin Cities Dunkers.

The Twin Cities Dunkers was started as an offshoot of the Minneapolis Chamber of Commerce in the late 1940s. Today it has three hundred members and meets for breakfast at the Minneapolis Club about twenty times a year. The practice of dunking doughnuts into coffee cups has long since disappeared, but the list of high-profile guests is a constant. I've had the opportunity to run the organization since its founder, Norm McGrew, died in 2004.

Often, the best part of the meeting is when the guests share some of their favorite stories. Cincinnati Reds Hall of Fame catcher Johnny Bench appeared several years ago in conjunction with his appearance at a senior men's golf event at the TPC Club. Most of the questions were about baseball.

He spoke about growing up in a small Oklahoma town where his father was widely known as the region's best athlete.

Every Saturday, the senior Bench would position his son in front of the television set to watch the *Major League Baseball Game of the Week*.

"It was pretty common for Dad to explode out of his chair at least two or three times a game, knock over his beer bottle, and yell at the TV, 'Geez, even I could hit that one,'" Bench said with a laugh.

As Bench tells it, he wasn't the best high school student, so when he was drafted by the Reds in June 1965, there was little debate about whether he would sign a contract.

He rose rapidly through the Cincinnati's minor league system and in 1967 received a late-season call-up to the majors. He earned a spot as the team's everyday catcher as soon as he arrived.

In 1968, Bob Gibson of the St. Louis Cardinals put together one of the best seasons ever by a major league pitcher. In mid June, Bench and the Reds traveled to St. Louis to face Gibson and the Cardinals. Bench vividly recalled his first at-bat against Gibson.

Strike one was safely in the catcher's glove before Bench even thought about swinging. He fouled the second pitch in the dirt around home plate and feebly swung late and missed on strike three.

Walking back to the Reds dugout, he had a strange smile on his face. It wasn't the look that his manager, Dave Bristol, wanted to see.

"Bench," Bristol yelled at his young catcher, "would you mind telling us what's so god-damned funny about striking out on three pitches?"

Bench told him the only thing he could think of—the truth.

"Dad couldn't hit this guy," he said.

Puckett's Neighborhood

The third time I saw Kirby Puckett walking across the undeveloped lot next to our Edina home, I went outside to talk to him.

The lot was one of the last available lakefront properties in Edina, and I had heard that the popular Twin was thinking of moving from his home in the north suburbs.

"Are you going buy this lot?" I asked him.

"Hey, big guy, I don't think so."

"Why not? It's a great lot."

"You're right about that, man, but the guy who owns it wants too much for it."

"Tell me you don't like the neighbors or it's too close to the highway, but don't tell me you can't afford it."

"Man, it don't matter how much money you got. If something's overpriced, it's still too much money."

He lowered his voice and got serious.

"And besides, you don't want me for a next-door neighbor," he continued. "Once the word got out that Kirby Puckett lives here, there'd be cars driving around this cul-de-sac night and day. You'd get to hate it. I'm looking at another lot on the other side of the lake. It's got a long driveway and the house would be invisible from the street. That's a better deal all around."

He could see that I was disappointed.

"Why would you want me for a next-door neighbor?" he asked.

"I want to be the answer to a trivia question," I told him honestly.

"What's that? What local sports guy lives next to Kirby Puckett?"

"No. Better than that. Who is the only family in Edina with black neighbors on both sides?"

Kirby said he loved the question, but he did build about a mile away a home that was totally invisible from the street. There was no name on the mailbox. He did show up on the sidelines when his kids competed in sports, and his house was a popular Halloween stop for neighborhood children.

The neighbors on the other side of us were Noah and Rena Hurley. Noah was a successful entrepreneur, and Rena was a realtor who specialized in finding housing for many black athletes who were new to Minnesota.

The Hurleys had moved into their new house several months before we moved into ours. On our second night in the neighborhood, Noah was at our door with some homemade chili. He and his wife frequently entertained a number of the Minnesota Vikings after games. He would often call and invite us to come over. If there were leftovers, Noah would appear at our door, food in hand, hoping we hadn't eaten dinner yet.

I would see Kirby from time to time in the neighborhood. He always had a friendly greeting and told me how lucky we were not to have him as a neighbor. Kirby was true to his word about keeping a low profile.

The local Davanni's Pizza was owned and operated by three long-time friends of mine, Bob Carlson, Mick Stenson, and Roger Schelper. On nights that Linda and I were in a hurry for dinner, I would call ahead and place my order.

One night I walked in to Davanni's and announced that I was there to pick up a pizza for Dave. Three other customers were sitting and reading newspapers while waiting for their takeout orders.

As the cashier was handing me my pizza, I heard a voice from behind one of the papers say, "That's not fair, man. You just got here and we've all been waiting for our pizzas."

I recognized the voice behind the newspaper.

"Kirby," I said, "I always call ahead. I've got the number programmed on our phone."

"Thanks, man," he replied. "I'm always starving when I'm sitting here. I'm calling ahead from now on."

When Kirby was inducted into the Hall of Fame in 2001, we struck a deal with him to sign a number of bats, balls, gloves, and photos for us to sell in our Field of Dreams memorabilia store at the Mall of America. Kirby would show up at our Eden Prairie warehouse and sign for several hours at a time. He never seemed to be in any hurry to leave and was always talkative on a variety of subjects. He also displayed a nice sense of humor.

We always wanted Kirby to sign bats and photos with sharp, new pens. Usually a pen was good for twenty-five to thirty signatures before it needed to be replaced. One day he showed up when we were short on new pens.

Beth Lorie, who worked with Linda in the office, asked Kirby if he was all right with staying alone while she drove to the store for new pens.

"No problem," he said, "if you trust me."

She was back twenty-five minutes later. The office was wide open, and there was no sign of Puckett.

"Kirby," she called. There was no answer.

She tried the warehouse. Again, no answer.

Finally, she yelled, "Kirby, I know you're in there because your car is still parked out front."

"OK," he responded, stepping out from behind some framing materials, "you got me on that one—but I had you worried."

Several months after Kirby died in 2006, we sorted through the unsold inventory of what he had signed over that period of weeks.

At the bottom of a large stack of signed sixteen- by twenty-inch photos, we found that he had personalized a photo to each of his kids, Kirby Jr. and Catherine, telling them he loved them. We were able to get them to them shortly after their father's death.

Bob Feller vs. Michelle Tafoya

Linda and I opened our first Field of Dreams sports memorabilia store at the Mall of America in August 1992. We were the first franchise owners within the chain, and we eventually owned seven stores in the Twin Cities, Seattle, Indianapolis, Philadelphia, and Springfield, Missouri. Over the years we had a chance to meet many legends from the world of sports.

But no one was quite like Bob Feller.

The former Cleveland Indians star is now one of the three oldest living members of the Baseball Hall of Fame. He's made far more money over his lifetime signing his name than he ever did throwing a baseball more than 95 miles per hour.

At a time when many Hall of Famers were charging upward of $10,000 for a two-hour autograph session, Feller charged $2,500.

"Those guys who charge $10,000 sign maybe three or four times a year," he said with a laugh. "I can work every day of every weekend. Now who's the fool?"

We brought Bob to the Mall of America on three different occasions. My favorite was his first trip here, in 1993.

At the time, we had three stores: at Ridgedale, Galleria, and Mall of America. We planned a full day for Bob. He was to start signing in the morning at Ridgedale, have lunch with key customers, sign in the afternoon at Galleria, have dinner with key customers, and sign in the early evening at the Mall of America.

I picked him up at the airport early in the morning and explained the schedule.

"That's perfect," he said. "You've got me for the whole day. Let's get to work."

He asked if there was anything else, and I told him that he would be doing a radio interview to build interest in the evening signings.

"I like radio," he said. "What station am I going to be on?"

"KFAN," I said. "It's one of those all-sports stations that are starting to pop up around the country."

Me and Linda with Bob Feller at the Field of Dreams store at the Mall of America, 1993

"I've done a lot of those shows. Who am I going to be talking to?"

I hesitated briefly before answering.

"Michele Tafoya."

"A broad?" he barked, reminding me of his distinguished background in the U.S. Navy. "I'm going to be interviewed by a broad?"

"Don't worry about Michele," I assured him. "She'll have done her homework. I'm sure it'll be a great interview."

He was quiet for a few seconds before replying.

"You seem like a smart young guy, and I'm inclined to trust you. But if she asks me what position I played, the goddamn interview is over."

Tafoya, as usual, was well prepared. She walked him through his career, asked him about his time serving his country in World War II, and concluded with his thoughts on Pete Rose's qualifications for the Baseball Hall of Fame (over Bob's dead body).

Shortly after the Feller interview, Tafoya moved on to a national market and, most recently, has worked NBA games for ABC and served as a sideline reporter for ESPN's *Monday Night Football*.

"I'll Have One of Me"

One sale in our years at the Field of Dreams stores stands out above all others. It wasn't because of the amount of the sale—it was only $39.99—but it was one of the strangest.

The Cleveland Indians were in Minnesota for a series with the Twins. As was often the case on off days or on days before night games, some of the visiting players made their way to the Mall of America. Carlos Baerga, then the Cleveland second baseman, came in to the store with a young woman.

After checking out the various displays, the woman found something she wanted.

Laughing, Carlos Baerga paid forty dollars for an autographed eight-by ten-inch framed photo of Carlos Baerga.

A Day with the Champ

Linda and I have had a chance to sit through lengthy autograph sessions with the likes of Dan Marino, Harmon Killebrew, Paul Hornung, Duke Snider, Roger Clemens, Pete Rose, Ralph Branca, Bobby Thomson, Ted "Double-Duty" Radcliffe, Sam Jethroe, Buck O'Neill, and Bob Feller, as well as the fifty greatest basketball players in the history of the National Basketball Association, including Larry Bird, Magic Johnson, and Michael Jordan.

But Muhammad Ali was something special.

We arranged a private eight-hour signing session with him at a hotel in Anaheim in 1998. His advancing Parkinson's made it difficult for him to sign autographs, but he was a good sport, at more than $250 per signature. He would hold the pen in his right hand while someone placed the photo beneath the spot where he was to sign. We all took turns at being the person to slide the photos in and out.

Ali seldom spoke, but he missed nothing as he signed. From time to time, my wife would ask, "How about a couple of Cassius Clays, champ?"

He'd smile, and the next four or five would carry the seldom-seen Clay autograph.

Every sixty to ninety minutes, the Champ would take a break. He'd stand, flex his fingers, and invite customers to another part of the room for photos.

Ali always worked with the same photographer, and they were a perfect team. Looking for the most innocent candidate, Ali would beckon the person to move in for a close-up.

Putting his chin within inches of his unsuspecting victim, he'd whisper, "Did you just call me nigger?" Feigning shock, he'd raise his fist and glare at his victim, the photographer capturing the moment before the person could realize that he or she was being set up.

As with nearly everything else he did, nobody did photos better than Ali.

The Champ, Muhammad Ali, puts his signature to a pile of boxing gloves.

The Fifty Greatest

The first time I heard the idea I thought it was an outrageous amount of money. Field of Dreams had approached the National Basketball Association about creating a limited-edition lithograph to be signed by the forty-nine living members of the players voted as the fifty greatest from the first fifty years of the league.

Sam Battistone and his business partner, Joie Casey, had conceptualized the Field of Dreams retail store idea in 1990. Prior to that, Battistone had been co-owner of the Utah Jazz and was a close friend of NBA Commissioner David Stern. When Battistone and Casey heard that the NBA was going to celebrate its fiftieth anniversary with the selection of an all-time team, they approached the commissioner with the idea to create a commemorative lithograph and to generate a substantial sum of money to be made available to players who finished their careers before the establishment of adequate pension programs.

Stern bought into the plan and invited Field of Dreams store owners to be guests of the NBA in Cleveland, site of the Fiftieth Anniversary All-Star Celebration weekend in 1997. It made the most sense to have the 250 lithographs signed there, because many of the fifty players would be in uniform, and the others were to be honored guests of the league for the days leading up to the all-star game itself.

Each player was to receive a signed litho. The league retained one hundred pieces. Field of Dreams got the remaining hundred. In order to cover the costs of the project and have enough left over for the retired players' fund, each lithograph needed to sell for $25,000, an unheard of price in sports collectables at the time. It was by far the largest amount of money ever asked for a created piece of sports memorabilia. Babe Ruth's bat, Lou Gehrig's uniform, and Honus Wagner's rare baseball card had sold for more, but this was a new level for sports art.

The justification for the argument was based on the fact that only one hundred of the signed lithographs would be available for retail sale, and that these high-profile athletes had never before signed anything of this magnitude. There also was no question of the lithograph's authenticity, given the full and enthusiastic participation of the NBA.

At the time the deal was signed, no one had any idea what the makeup of the team would be. As it turned out, forty-nine of the fifty players selected were still living. Only Pete Maravich was deceased.

The completed but unsigned lithographs, bearing the likenesses of the fifty players, were shipped to a Cleveland hotel to be signed. All the retired players were staying at that hotel, and a signing schedule was established.

Five tables were set up for signing, and each table was assigned a stack of fifty lithos. The lithos moved from table to table, but the players stayed put. The autographs were all done in pencil, and pencils were changed every twenty autographs to ensure a fine point. All the women assisting on the signing were told to remove any fingernail polish, and we all constantly washed our hands to avoid smudges and fingerprints.

The fastest signers took about twenty minutes to sign 250 lithographs. The average was closer to fifty minutes. Paul Arizin, a natural right hander who had suffered a stroke, took two and a half hours, signing every lithograph deliberately and perfectly with his left hand.

John Stockton was among the first to arrive, and he came back to the room several times with his young sons. Jerry Lucas, the former New York Knicks and Cincinnati Royals forward from Ohio State, was among the first signers, and he hung around for most of the three days to visit with former teammates and opponents he hadn't seen in years. During his playing days, Lucas would amaze his teammates with tricks such as memorizing the New York telephone directory.

League pioneers such as George Mikan were treated with the greatest respect by the younger selectees.

The first player in the first group that we worked with was Boston Celtic great John Havlicek. I commented on his flawlessly clear signature and told him it looked familiar. "You ever take a close look at the Declaration of Independence?" he asked. "From the first time I saw that John Hancock signature and realized how similar our names were, I knew that was the way I wanted to sign my name."

Maravich's name appears without a signature, but his family stopped by numerous times to visit and to hear stories about their father.

Julius Erving had fingers so long and elegant they made the pencil nearly disappear. He received special deference from the other players.

234

Former Celtic teammates Bob Cousy and Bill Sharman showed up at the same time and commented on how amazed they had been when they heard that teammate Bill Russell had agreed to sign.

"There was a time when Bill Russell's autograph was supposed to be as hard to get as the pope's and Fidel Castro's," Cousy said. "I don't remember ever seeing him sign anything. I wonder if he'll show."

Russell showed up later that afternoon and was pleasant throughout the signing.

Several years earlier, Don Nelson, a one-time teammate of Russell's and at that time the Celtics coach, had taken a bus from his downtown Minneapolis hotel to our store at the Mall of America to purchase a basketball signed by Russell. "I always wanted a team ball," he said, "but Bill wouldn't sign one. Now I can get the other guys and build my team ball around Bill's signature."

The first signer on the second morning was Wilt Chamberlain. There have been taller players in the history of the league, but I've never seen one with longer legs.

All fifty players had been promised that they would not be asked to sign additional autographs. As a result, most of them were more than happy to pose for photos. Few of the men in our group stood much more than chest high on Chamberlain, and it was hard to get a close-up photo showing both heads. A few months earlier, he had written a book in which he claimed to have slept with some 20,000 women. The women in our group refused to be photographed with

Wilt, either out of disrespect or fear that someone might misinterpret the occasion.

As the second day wound down, rumors were circulating that Larry Bird was balking on signing. From the start, he had shown no interest in the project, and he missed his first two signing slots. Former teammate Kevin McHale and commissioner Stern were recruited to deliver the reluctant Celtic. Word came back that Bird wanted to know if Magic Johnson and Michael Jordan had signed yet. It was beginning to look as if our only chance with Jordan would be on game day, and that meant that Johnson and Bird also would be late signers.

On the third day, we got a police escort to move the lithographs to the ballroom of the hotel where the active players were staying.

With Wilt Chamberlain for the signing event with the NBA's top 50 players

Clyde Drexler and Robert Parish were the first to show up. We were set up in an enormous room with about a football field's worth of empty space between us and the far side of the room. One of the owners had brought his two young sons to observe, but they were under orders not to approach the players.

Minutes later, Charles Barkley burst into the room.

"This must be the place," he said. "Let's get going."

Sitting alongside Drexler, he spotted Parish several tables away, signing silently.

"Hey, Chief," he yelled, evoking Parish's nickname. "What was it like to play against Mikan?"

"You know I'm not that old," Parish replied.

"Can't tell it by the way you look," Barkley laughed and resumed signing.

He would sign about a dozen and roll his shoulders and flex his fingers. "I'm sore," he told us. "This is hard work."

My wife, sensing an opening with the playful Barkley, said, "What you need is a good backrub."

"I'm available," he dared.

Seconds later, he was benefiting from a solid shoulder rub.

"Excuse us," he said, "we'll be up in my room for the next couple of hours."

"I'd like you to meet my husband," she said. "He's the one with the sharp pencils."

"OK, time to get back to signing," he laughed.

Even after he finished signing the 250 lithographs, Barkley was in no hurry to leave. He asked when he would be getting his finished litho, and how the money was going to be used. He stood by while others signed and critiqued their handwriting.

Finally, he realized it was time to go, but not before he had a little more fun.

Moving as quietly as a man his size could, he came up behind one of the young boys playing quietly on the far side of the room. In one quick move he picked up the nine-year-old and spun him overhead three or four times before lowering him gently to the floor.

"That'll give him something to tell his friends about," he grinned and was gone out the door.

The NBA All-Star Game was being played the next night, and we had all but four players' signatures. Shaquille O'Neal was injured and had not traveled to Cleveland, so he was going to sign later. We were missing Magic Johnson, Larry Bird, and Michael Jordan.

Commissioner Stern said the NBA had arranged for a police escort to take us from the hotel to the arena. We had a small room in Cleveland's Gund Arena and a promise from the commissioner that we would have all three signed before the opening tip-off.

"Be ready," he said, "because you won't be getting much advance notice."

Johnson arrived first and could not have been friendlier. He shook hands all around and talked throughout the twenty-five minutes he took to sign. Upon leaving, he thanked us for what we were doing for the retired players and said he already has a spot in mind for his litho.

Jordan was next. He was escorted by a half dozen guards who called out, "Michael is coming. Everybody stand back. He's coming. He's coming."

He walked into the room, picked up a pencil, and went to work.

"Michael," Joie Casey said, "do you mind if we take some pictures while you sign?"

Jordan looked up briefly, nodded his assent and went back to work. We each took turns moving in closely behind him while he signed one litho after another. Seventeen minutes later, and without saying a word, he was on his feet and ready to rejoin the action in the arena.

We were still missing Bird. Commissioner Stern said that we needed to come back right before the game and that Bird would be the last to sign.

"Let's get this over with," was all he said when he arrived, making no pretense about any enthusiasm for the project. Casey, sensing that Bird would have little interest in the completed piece, said to him: "Larry, we know you're not crazy about this, and we really appreciate your doing this. I'd be happy to write you a check right here for $25,000 for your litho if you'd consider selling it." Bird accepted on the spot, and Casey wound up with the lithograph entitled, Bird 1 of 1.

As the game got underway, we boxed up the lithos and took them under police escort to the airport.

Since the completion of the project several more players have died, including Mikan, Chamberlain, and Dave DeBusschere.

The customers who paid $25,000 for a fully signed piece had made a decent purchase. The most recent sales, nearly a decade later, were in the $62,000 to $75,000 range.

Michael Jordan adds his signature to the poster of the top 50 players.

A Fire Next Time

By far, the question I get asked most frequently is: "What is Sid Hartman really like?"

The second most common question I get is: "Aren't you the guy who lost all those baseball cards in that big flood we had back in 1987?"

It's amazing how that story remains after two decades, but I still think about it every time I hear a thunderstorm.

On July 20, 1987, most of the Minneapolis/St. Paul area received between three and four inches of rain. It was welcome at a time when precipitation was below normal and lawns and golf courses were turning prematurely brown. Although the driving rains filled ditches, small streams, and lakes, they presented only the normal problems that accompany that amount of rain in a short period of time.

What none of us knew was that the first storm was merely a preview of what was to follow.

The forecast for July 24 was for heavy rain over most of the state. A lingering hot-air current to the east was going to be rammed by a cold front from the northwest, and it was all supposed to occur somewhere over central Minnesota.

The forecasters were right on.

The rain moved into the metropolitan area with a tornado touch-down in Maple Grove. Just as we were watching the live coverage on local television, the same dark clouds rolled over our house. Even though we were only four weeks removed from the longest day of the year, it grew dark as heavy rain clouds moved in. Eventually the clouds merged into one dark mass, and it began to pour.

The ground was totally saturated from the rain of the previous days, and a pond began to form outside our lower-level garage door. We heard the familiar sound of the sump pump, which we had put in after having the garage floor flooded by several earlier rains over the ten years we'd lived in the house.

We were just commenting that we had never seen it rain that hard for that long when the TV weatherman introduced us to a new word, "entrainment." The storm was pulling more unstable air into itself and continually regenerating over the same area. It could be a long, wet night, he warned.

Again, we went downstairs to look outside. The pond above the sump pump was growing, and water was beginning to cover the garage floor, just a large step below the lower level of our house. Of greater concern was the rapidly growing lake that was forming in a low spot on the lawn of our backyard. That area was separated from the house by a good-size berm, but if the water went over the berm, we knew we were going to be in trouble.

We began checking the water level every five minutes, spending the rest of the time looking at the television radar display for any hint of a break.

A little more than an hour after the rain began, water began oozing into the lower level of the house from below the four sliding doors that led to the backyard. The berm had been breached, and a small river was headed toward the back of the house.

The lower level of the house consisted of a laundry room, my baseball card office, a large family room, and a huge storage room that contained everything from wedding photos and scrapbooks to out-of-season clothes, suitcases, tools, toys, and cleaning supplies.

Counting the four-drawer file in the entryway, my room full of cards, and what I stored in the backroom, I had more than one million baseball, football, basketball, and hockey cards dating back to the turn of the twentieth century.

Sensing that the rain couldn't get much worse, we began moving things on that level to higher ground. Desktops quickly were filled, as were the Ping-Pong table and the top of the Genie pinball machine that we had purchased several weeks earlier. Surely the water could not get up to thirty-six inches. Once again we were wrong.

Quickly, my wife; our two sons, Erik and Kirk; and a neighbor, Rich Powell, formed a line up the stairs as we began moving things of value to the upper level of the house.

With the water now knee deep, Linda and the three boys—who were eleven to thirteen years of age at the time—went to work in the storage room while I continued with the more valuable cards. Suddenly I remembered that we had two cars parked in the garage and the water would be more than knee deep in a few minutes. I raced up the stairs to get both sets of car keys and ran back down.

I pressed the button to open the overhead garage door, thankful that the electricity was still working.

I rapidly backed my car through the rising waves and around the floating law furniture. I drove through accumulating water about a block and a half to the west, where I parked the car in a church lot that was some twenty feet above the level of our house. I ran back home and quickly backed my wife's car out just before our front deck floated loose from its moorings and blocked the driveway.

With the water now waist deep in the entire lower level, and well over the electrical outlets, we knew it was time to forget about the yearbooks and remaining baseball cards. We watched as, one by one, each of the sliding glass doors into the lower level loudly exploded under the weight of the onrushing water.

Just then we heard pounding on our front door. We ran to the door and found a young man who said his car was going underwater in front of our house, and he needed help to move it. The five of us were able to push his Porsche convertible to slightly higher ground. (It was towed away the next day, and we later heard that it was beyond repair.)

Minutes after we had taken care of the motorist, we heard another, more panicked knock at the front door. It was Marit Parten, the high school–age girl from next door, dressed in a T-shirt and shorts and bleeding profusely from a deep gash on her calf.

Marit and one of her friends had been badly cut when a window shattered in their house. There seemed no chance that an ambulance could get to us on the flooded streets, so we and another set of neighbors worked to carry the two girls to the local fire station, less than two blocks away, through the rising waters.

The station was filled with people who had abandoned their cars underwater on Highway 62, but the two girls were the only ones with serious injuries. An ambulance from Fairview Southdale Hospital was finally able to plow through the flooded streets and take them to the hospital. Although they lost a lot of blood, there was no lasting damage.

It was nearly one o'clock in the morning when I left the fire station. The rain was letting up, and by 2 a.m. it had stopped.

The official weather station at the airport reported 7.8 inches of rain in about four hours, breaking a ninety-five-year-old record for the most rain in a single day. The gauge at the fire station showed 14.4 inches of rain.

Highways 35W, 494, and 62 were all closed, with major sections under water. Southdale and Ridgedale malls were havens for hundreds of stranded shoppers who fled to upper levels as rain poured into below-grade stores. A Hopkins man died when he was swept away in a swift current, and a South Minneapolis man was killed when his basement wall collapsed on top of him. Governor Perpich declared the entire state a disaster area until officials could sort out the places most affected.

Slowly and for the next year, we were in the throes of rebuilding.

During the deluge, I had called into WCCO Radio to give an eyewitness account. I must have mentioned the baseball card collection, and a photographer from the *Star Tribune* stopped by the next day to take pictures of me setting some of my more valuable cards out to dry on what was left of our front walkway.

The story and photo ran on the front page of the next day's paper. A retired librarian saw the story, looked us up in the telephone directory, and called to say that the library had some success with freezing valuable documents that had been flooded.

It was some of the best unsolicited advice I ever got. As soon as power was restored, we threw away the rotting side of beef that we had recently purchased and replaced it with stacks and stacks of semi-precious baseball cards. The cards were damaged, but not nearly as bad as the ones that never saw the inside of our freezer.

Friends arrived with brooms and deli trays. One neighbor who we barely knew did our laundry until we had a new washer and dryer hooked up. We worked each day on cleanup and went to our office building to shower and change clothes in the workout area each night.

Four or five days after the flood, I remembered that I had taken out a special $20,000 insurance policy on the baseball card collection. I called the agent and he said they would have someone out the next day.

"You'll need to get the cards into an area where he can take some pictures to assess the damage," he explained. "Then he'll take them away, and we'll write you a check."

My family and friends worked for hours, carting nineteen wheelbarrows full of soggy, rotting cardboard to the top of our driveway. It formed a pile about four feet across, three feet high, and twelve feet long.

The appraiser arrived early the next morning. He was driving a Datsun that was maybe fifty percent as large as the pile of cards. Armed with a Polaroid camera, he took pictures from several angles and kept muttering under his breath.

"I've got what I need," he said, after no more than three minutes. "If you can come with me to my car, I'll write you a check and I'll be on my way and you folks can go back to your cleanup."

He handed me a check for $20,000, the full amount of the policy. The total loss on cards alone was $120,000.

"I thought you were going to take them away," I said. "That's what they told me on the phone."

"Look at what I'm driving," he protested. "I don't think the guy on the phone had any idea about the volume we were talking about."

"What are we supposed to do with them now?" I asked.

"It's up to you. I've seen all I need to see." And he drove away.

Later that day, all the neighborhood kids came to check out the huge pile of baseball cards. I was working in the yard.

"Hey, mister," more than one of them said. "What are you going to do with all these cards?"

"Either throw them away or give them away, I guess. Do you want some?"

It was an offer they couldn't refuse. In minutes they were back with the first containers they could find: paper grocery sacks.

The kids loaded up the bags before I could change my mind, then took off for home with their new treasures. On average it took less than a block for the bottom to fall out of the bags. There were trails of baseball cards throughout the neighborhood for the better part of a week.

For years our family didn't talk much about the night of the flood. Our boys came to our bedroom to sleep through every thunderstorm in the next year. Our older son, Erik, still claims that he had the high score on the Genie pinball machine, but the only evidence lies at the bottom of a landfill somewhere.

Weeks after the flood, our boys were leafing through a copy of *Weekly World News* while we were in the checkout line at the local supermarket.

"You're not going to believe this," they said, pointing to an article that read, "1.5 Million Soaked."

Until that day, I always assumed that magazine made up all its news.

Nicknames

I had been broadcasting Gopher football on WCCO Radio for about a decade and watching it for parts of four decades when someone asked me what were some of the biggest changes I'd seen in the sport over the years.

I'm guessing they were looking for an answer that talked about the change in size or speed of the athletes or the development of the pass-oriented offenses, but I said the first thing that popped into my mind: There are hardly any good nicknames anymore.

Think about it. The college and professional football historical landscape is littered with great nicknames. Nearly half the members of the pro and collegiate halls of fame boast nicknames. Somewhere along the way, however, football turned its back on the drop kick, the flying wedge, the lonesome end—and nicknames.

It's pretty much the same story in baseball and basketball. Where are the "Rabbit" Maranvilles, "Three-Finger" Browns, "PeeWee" Reeses, Wilt "the Stilt" Chamberlains, "Sweetwater" Cliftons, and "Hondo" Havliceks?

I looked back over fifty years of football history for evidence. Many fans would claim no first-hand knowledge of the game of half a century ago—until they hear the names. In speaking engagements I throw out a name and ask for the nickname. I get twenty-somethings shouting out the nicknames.

Joe "the Jet" Perry

Leo "the Lion" Nomellini

Norm "the Dutchman" Van Brocklin

Vito "Babe" Parelli

Edmund "Zeke" Bratkowski

Elroy "Crazy Legs" Hirsch

Floyd "Breezy" Reid

Charlie "Choo-Choo" Justice

Howard "Hopalong" Cassidy

Claude "Buddy" Young

Ewell "Doak" Walker

Lou "the Toe" Groza

Hugh "the King" McElhenny

Frank "Bucko" Kilroy

Harry "Chick" Jagade

"Deacon" Dan Towler

Paul "Tank" Younger

Dick "Night Train" Lane

Alan "the Horse" Ameche

Every one of those players was active fifty years ago.

Look a little deeper into the Hall of Fame and you find "Slingin'" Sammy Baugh, Byron "Whizzer" White, Frank "Bruiser" Kinard, and Wilbur "Fats" Henry, who weighed a mere (by today's standards) 230 pounds.

Look at the Gopher record books and you will quickly find Vernal "Babe" Levoir, W. W. "Pudge" Heffelfinger, Francis "Pug" Lund, George "Sonny" Franck, and Bronislau "Bronko" Nagurski, not to mention the "Butches," Larson and Nash, and the "Buds," Wilkinson and Grant.

Where are all the Fatsos, the Shorties, the Germans, the Swedes, and the Frenchies? Probably victims of political correctness.

Where are the Four Horsemen? The Seven Blocks of Granite? Mr. Inside and Mr. Outside?

Halloweens come and go with no mention of the Galloping Ghost. The Wheaton Iceman has been replaced by Kitchen Aide.

Oh, sure, there have been a few great nicknames in the past twenty-five years. We've had "Broadway Joe," "Sweetness," "Too Tall," the "Refrigerator," "Mean Joe," "White Shoes," and "The Stork." But by and large, nicknames are a vestige of the days of the single-wing formation.

Naming Opportunities

A lot has been written recently about the emergence of naming rights for stadiums as a way for amateur and professional teams to generate additional dollars. The concept has been around for two decades or more and is generally accepted as anything from a brilliant marketing scheme to a necessary evil.

In this market we've seen the Target Center and Xcel Energy Center. Beginning in 2009, the University of Minnesota will feature TCF Bank Stadium for the Gophers football team.

My wife and I were watching a preseason basketball game at the University of Minnesota when a thought occurred to me: An entire category of naming opportunities is out there just waiting to be explored.

The Gophers' opponents that afternoon were the Creighton University Bluejays. Why the Bluejays? Are the birds the dominant species in the Omaha area? Did the team once have an objectionable, politically incorrect nickname? There was obviously a reason for it, but there was also a huge opportunity going to waste.

In this day and age, imagine how much the school could gain if it was to negotiate with a certain retailer for the opportunity to rename their team the Creighton Barrels? Shouldn't it be worth a few million for all that exposure in the sports media? Headline writers across the country would have a field day with that one.

But why stop there? There are literally hundreds of colleges and universities in the nation that offer an opportunity to move into the twenty-first century of nicknames—and maybe make a few bucks along the way.

How about the Waldorf Salads? Although it may not strike fear in the hearts of opponents, it certainly is more memorable than the Waldorf Warriors, which must be on somebody's objectionable hit list.

For that matter, we could have the Emory Boards, the Briar Cliff Notes, the Ball State Jars, the Ferris Wheels, and the Rhodes Scholars.

We even have room for some of those collective nouns, words that don't have to end in an "s," much like the Minnesota Swarm or Minnesota Wild and the late Chicago Fire.

We could have the Cumberland Gap (don't you think a certain clothing company would like that one?), the Hastings Battle, the Louisiana Purchase, and the Maine Remembrance.

The James Madison Dollys is gender challenged. The Austin Peay Shooters may be in questionable taste, and I wouldn't begin to mess with Oral Roberts.

I would, however, make a strong argument for the Kent State Kryptonites, Navy Seals, Army Brats, Rice Krispies, Yale Locks, Converse Sneakers, Harvey Mudd Hens, Brown Derbys, Bradley Tanks, York Mints, Webb Crawlers, and Bowling Green Hornets.

At least half those new nicknames should have some strong financial implications. Instead of going to the college alumni or state legislature for more money, maybe it's time for some of these schools to be just a little more creative.

Optimistic Canadian

Every year, the organization Achieve!Minneapolis, for which I serve on the board of directors, holds one major public event, and in 2007, the featured speaker was a man named Geoffrey Canada. As news of the speaker spread, the event, held on the fiftieth floor of the IDS Tower, quickly sold out. I was among the few who did not know of Canada, and I was in for a treat.

Geoffrey Canada runs the Harlem Children's Zone, an organization that has achieved remarkably positive results in educating kids in a hundred-square-block area of Harlem in New York City.

It took about thirty seconds for Canada to enchant the audience with tales of his multiple appearances on *60 Minutes* and a nerve-racking appearance on *Oprah*.

Listening to Canada, it was obvious that there was a direct line between his vision, drive, and charisma and the program's impressive outcomes in an area where other efforts to improve the educational system had failed.

"I've spent most of my life in New York City," he said, "and I've thought a lot about why some neighborhoods thrive while others fail. I've come to an interesting conclusion. There is a tremendous gravity to these neighborhoods. You can rise above things for a short period of time, but eventually this gravity will pull you back. What's missing is a sense of optimism. Why do your homework if you don't expect to live to see your twentieth birthday?

Why go to school if there are no parents in your home and the most popular person in the neighborhood is the local drug dealer? There is a tremendous feeling of despair and lack of hope for the future."

Canada went on to say that almost everyone who has ever spent time with him remarks on his optimism. Where others see only gloom, he sees opportunity. His father played no significant role in his upbringing, and he asked himself where this optimism started.

His answer surprised everyone in the audience and became a topic for one of my Gopher football pregame essays. His optimism started with his high school football coach. Here's how he told the story.

He was the junior quarterback on a senior-dominated team in the South Bronx that was one of the best in New York City. Very few members of his class played football, so in his senior year the team featured mostly sophomores and juniors.

"What do you think?" his coach asked him on the first day of summer practice that senior season.

"We're pretty small," Canada observed.

"You're right, Geoffrey," the coach said, "but small teams tend to be fast, and I've got a whole set of plays for small, fast guys."

Satisfied, Canada quarterbacked the team in their first game, which they lost. Turned out they were not only small, but they were slow, too.

"I know that," the coach explained, "but other teams won't know that. They'll see that we aren't very big, and they'll set up their defenses to stop small, fast guys. I've got a whole offense designed for small, slow guys who look like they're fast. Trust me."

So, Canada led the team to losses in games two, three, and four.

The season was now half over, and Canada was openly discouraged. His coach noticed and tried to reassure him.

"These kids are new to the system, and it takes about half a year to figure things out. That's all behind us now. We're at the point of the year when all that hard work is about to pay off. They just need you to get out there and lead them."

Canada did his best, but the team lost games five, six, and seven. Their eighth and final game was against the team that was leading the conference with a perfect 7-0 record. It wasn't hard to antici-pate the outcome, and Canada lingered in front of his locker with kickoff approaching.

"What's wrong?" his coach asked.

"We're gonna get killed out there. We don't have a chance against these guys."

"Listen, this is your chance of a lifetime. Most people would kill for this. Fifty years from now people will still be talking about the last-place team that upset the best team in New York. Some people wait their entire lives and never have an opportunity like this, and it's right in front of you. You get to be the quarterback who engineered the upset of the century. Now get your pads on and go out and make it happen."

Energized, Canada slipped into his gear and led the team to their eighth and final loss of the season.

Sitting at his locker after the game, he couldn't wait to hear what the coach had to say, but he wanted to go first.

"Coach, all year long you were telling us we were going to win, that this would be the week. So we went out there and lost every single game. I just can't see what there is to be so optimistic about."

Putting his arm around the quarterback, the coach leaned in close, smiled, and said, "But, Geoffrey, basketball season starts Monday!"

And that's why there's hope today for those kids in a hundred-square-block area in Harlem.

Marginally True

I flew with the Blue Angels, and my wife sang at Carnegie Hall.

Some years ago, Linda and I were invited to a dinner at which very few of the people knew one another, and virtually no one knew the spouses. The organizers planned to kick off the cocktail hour with a mixer in which the guests were challenged to learn something about one another. The assignment was simple. State a single fact about yourself that would amuse or astonish the other guests.

This wasn't the first time we'd played that game. For years we both used the fact that we had spent a day with Muhammad Ali. Linda admitted that she once showed cows at the Hennepin County Fair and once gave Charles Barkley a shoulder rub. I sold popcorn at Metropolitan Stadium and weighed 137 pounds when I graduated from high school (that one stumped them every time). But too many people at this upcoming event knew about our involvement in sports, and the Ali question might have been too obvious.

We supplied our clues a week in advance of the event. The night of the dinner we were greeted at the door with pens and alphabetized lists of attendees and facts. People looking for ex-Navy fliers quickly dismissed me as a candidate—but wait a minute.

Back in the mid 1960s, the Blue Angels were going to make a rare appearance in the Minneapolis/St. Paul area, and they were sending an advance plane to the region to stir up interest.

259

"Want to do something fun for a change?" asked *Tribune* assistant city editor Irv Letofsky.

"What do you have in mind?"

"The Blue Angels are coming here, and they're going to be doing some test flights with the media on Saturday. Looks like a pretty slow news day. I'll sign you up and you can do an advance. It's either that, or you can write the weather story and obits."

Faced with such an easy decision, I opted for the flight.

No, that's not me in the cockpit. This is a publicity photo for the Blue Angels.

It turns out that all the local television stations had signed up before me, and I was the last passenger of the day. I drove to the air base section of Minneapolis/St. Paul International Airport for my briefing. They found a flight suit in my size, and I got a quick tutorial on how to survive a high-speed ejection over Minnetonka.

After nearly two hours of waiting, it was my time to climb the steps into the passenger seat of a nasty-looking blue streak.

The pilot greeted me with a big, perfect smile. "A young guy," he observed. "You want the standard flight, or do you want to have some fun?"

There is only one acceptable answer to such a question.

"I'm not officially authorized to operate below five thousand feet, so I'll have to ask you to keep your eyes off the altimeter. Also, I need to ask you to write only about the official parts of the next few minutes."

Once the deal was struck, we took off over Richfield.

It was a hot summer day and the pilot was looking for a lake, preferably one with plenty of sailboats and bathing suits. He was describing Lake Minnetonka.

"Where is it from here?" he asked through the headset.

"About fifteen miles west of downtown Minneapolis on Highway 12," I told him.

"I have problems reading road signs from up here," he said with a laugh. "But if it's west of here and it's big, I'll find it."

What seemed like less than five minutes later, the pilot dropped the left wing and asked, "Does that look like it?"

It seemed too soon and too small to be Lake Superior, so I gave him an A for navigation.

"Let's take a closer look."

Dropping to five hundred feet, we buzzed the lake from Wayzata to Mound in a little more than a minute.

"That was great," I said, panting. "Incredible."

"You can see it even better this way," he said, rolling the plane onto its back.

Streaking at nearly four hundred miles an hour, we backtracked, capturing the attention of every bather and boater within miles.

After we landed a few minutes later, the pilot tested my memory.

"How'd you like the lake?" he said.

"What lake?" I responded. And that's the way I wrote it.

My wife's mystery story for the dinner party comes from the time that she and four friends visited New York for a long weekend.

Trying to see as many of the sights as possible, they hoped to take in a show at Carnegie Hall. When they got there, the venerable performance hall was dark. They told the only employee at the door that they had come all the way to New York to see Carnegie Hall (not true, but it was in keeping with what most New Yorkers feel about Minnesotans) and merely wanted to look inside.

"OK, go around to the side door and tell them Larry said it was all right to let you in."

Larry must have decided that this Minnesota group was no James Gang, and he let them in. "You can pretty much walk around and look at what you want to, but don't go onto the stage," he warned.

Linda couldn't resist. Standing inches in front of the stage, she sang the entire Italian aria that she had mastered in her many college voice lessons. The applause from her four friends was deafening, and they quickly agreed it was the best Carnegie Hall performance they had ever heard.

Who Was Tracy Stallard?
The Great Minnesota Sports Trivia Quiz

There is a fine line between trivia and minutia. A good trivia question should make you work hard to recall something that you once knew. Minutia can evoke the questions: Who knows? And who cares?

A baseball trivia buff may recall that Tracy Stallard threw the pitch that Roger Maris hit for his sixty-first home run in 1961. Minutia would be asking someone, who was the umpire in that game?

For six years from 1984 to 1989, our fledgling public relations firm, Mona & McGrath and later Mona Meyer McGrath & Gavin, ran an event called the Minnesota Sports Trivia Bowl, in partnership with WCCO Radio and the *Star Tribune*. At its peak, more than two hundred teams competed in the event.

For a chance to compete in the broadcast rounds, each four-person team would take a one-hundred-question qualifying quiz during a ninety-minute period at a local hotel or office building. The top qualifiers would meet in head-to-head, College Quiz Bowl–style competitions that were broadcast for an entire week on WCCO Radio. The ratings were outstanding, and the teams were impressive.

I worked for much of the year writing questions for both the quiz and radio rounds. Over the five years of the event, we used more than 6,500 questions, nearly all of which I still have on index cards. We would still be going today, but the teams got too good. Making the questions difficult enough to be hard work for the teams made the event less and less interesting for casual listeners.

Teams competing for the radio slots would arrive early and quiz one another from sources ranging from the Minnesota Vikings media guide to the ancient "Who's Who in the American Association." The competition was intense, and by quiz time the auditorium smelled like a locker room. The better teams were made up of experts in different fields. There were more questions about baseball than any other sport, but you had to know football, basketball, and hockey at the professional, college, and high school level—not to mention boxing, tennis, golf, and wrestling. It also paid to have someone who knew the history of sports in Minnesota. Also, there was always one or more spelling questions with names such as Nzigamasabo, Tschimperele, Ntsoelengoe, Navratilova, and Ericsson.

The final question was always a series of questions, the answers to which were to be multiplied, added, subtracted, and divided. Here's an example:

Take the number of former Minnesota Vikings in the Pro Football Hall of Fame; add the number of former Twins in the Baseball Hall of Fame; multiply by the number of teams in the NCAA postseason tournament field; add the last year in which the Lakers played basketball in Minneapolis; and subtract the highest number of home runs that Harmon Killebrew hit in a single year. What's your answer?

Back in 1986, the correct answer was 2,103.

I carried a note card with me wherever I went in case I thought of a possible question or answer. Often I would start with an answer and work backward into a question. Here's how that worked:

Answer: Hoyt Wilhelm.

Question: Name the former Minneapolis Miller who hit a home run in his first major league at-bat and, over a major league career that lasted more than twenty years, never hit another home run?

My favorite questions were those that could not be researched by any standard means. Among the quizzes, a single question still stands out: Name the Hall of Fame baseball player whose name appears on most batteries made in the United States. I could hear the groans sweep across the room when the teams first discovered and later solved that one. The answer: Al Kaline.

The night of the qualifying quiz, a number of our small staff and my wife and sons would grade them and rank them until early in the morning. Teams could call for their score and ranking beginning at 8:30 the next morning. We would hear from nearly every team in the first twenty minutes.

The radio rounds got to be the hardest to come up with questions for, as teams chewed through dozens of questions in a matter of minutes. Many of the contestants became friends. Mark Johnson was hired by the University of Minnesota sports information department to research pre–World War II football records. I later did a pregame feature on him as the man who literally rewrote the Gopher record book. His teammate, Don Timm, was elected to the University of Minnesota's Sports Hall of Fame as a distance runner. He could have easily made it years earlier as a trivia expert. John Gendler, a member of the champion Yankee Clippers, has had Twins seats directly in front of us since the opening of the Metrodome. At least twice a game he turns around to talk about one or more of the questions.

The HRD Selects team was made up of many of the best minds in the Minnesota House Research Division. These guys did research for a living, and they were formidable. The Hubies came from Hector, Minnesota, where captain John Huber was the newspaper editor.

Years after the competitions ended, I would meet people and begin to introduce myself. They'd interrupt me and say that we had met briefly in 1985 when their team had finished ninth in the Sports Trivia Bowl and would have finished in the top eight if they had listened to the guy who swore it was Lou Clinton who once threw out Earl Battey at first base on what looked like a sure single to right against the Red Sox.

What follows is an updated hundred-question quiz for people who think they know a thing or two about the local sports scene. Good luck.

Minnesota Sports Trivia Quiz

1. Who was the first manager of the Minnesota Twins?

2. What is Bud Grant's real first name?

3. The message board for the Minnesota Twins game at Metropolitan Stadium was known as what?

4. What Twins great was named for the doctor who delivered him on a train in Panama?

5. Name the tiny school that won the 1960 Minnesota Boys High School basketball championship, in the Minnesota equivalent of the movie *Hoosiers*.

6. Who was the winning pitcher against the Twins in game seven of the 1965 World Series?

7. What sport did the Minnesota Buckskins play?

8. The actual Hobey Baker Award statue was modeled after what former Gopher and U.S. Olympic hockey player?

9. Name the Minnesota resident who once won the Tour de France.

10. In University of Minnesota football history, who was the "Grey Eagle"?

11. Name the St. Paul native who pitched and won the final game of the 1991 World Series.

12. Name the Minnesota hometown of Minneapolis Laker Hall of Famer Vern Mikkelsen.

13. Which baseball Hall of Famer caught for the St. Paul Saints in the 1950s?

14. What former Gopher basketball player went straight from college to Major League Baseball in 1973?

15. Who, in an exhibition game, got the first base hit in the Metrodome?

16. Name the Minnesota Viking who returned a San Francisco 49er fumble the wrong way for a safety.

17. Paul Giel finished second in the Heisman Trophy voting to which Notre Dame back?

18. By what nickname is Austin's Bill Skowron better known?

19. Name perhaps the greatest trotting horse of all time, who came from Savage, Minnesota.

20. Who was the fictional "All-American Boy" who promoted Wheaties in the early days of radio?

21. Name the quarterback who once led Purdue to victory over the University of Minnesota and later returned to this state as the second baseman for the Twins.

22. Name the man who attended the University of Iowa briefly, played four years with the Harlem Globetrotters, and later starred for Pittsburgh and Minnesota in the American Basketball Association.

23. Who hit the first inside-the-park home run in Minnesota Twins history?

24. Who did Fran Tarkenton replace as quarterback in the first regular-season game in Minnesota Vikings history?

25. Name the Gopher running back who holds the Big Ten record with fifty-seven carries in a 1977 game against Illinois.

26. Name the only father/son combination to both rank in the top ten rushing yard totals for the Minnesota Gopher football team.

27. Janet Karvonan was perhaps the first great star of the Minnesota High School Girls Basketball Tournament. For what team did she play?

28. Name the only Minnesotan to ever win the Claret Jug.

29. What singing group attracted a record crowd of 65,000 to Metropolitan Stadium?

30. Does the University of Minnesota have a winning or a losing record against all of the following teams: Alabama, Arizona, Clemson, Iowa, Nebraska, Texas, UCLA, Washington, and Wisconsin?

31. The single-game basketball scoring record for Gopher basketball is forty-two points. That is the lowest single-game record in the Big Ten. It's shared by what two players?

32. Who scored the first regular-season goal in the history of Minnesota Wild hockey?

33. What professional golfer once said Hazeltine National Golf Course was missing eighty acres of corn and a few cows?

34. Name the Hutchinson, Minnesota, native who became a first-round draft choice in professional basketball.

35. Who preceded Terry Ryan as general manager of the Minnesota Twins?

36. What former Gopher once scored forty points in a single game for the expansion Minnesota Timberwolves?

37. Who owned the Minnesota North Stars when they became the Dallas Stars?

38. Name the St. Paul native who won the Heisman Trophy in 2000.

39. Name the former Gopher tight end who was inducted into the Pro Football Hall of Fame in 2007.

40. Name the former Gopher All-American who retired as a professional wrestling champion to try his hand at professional football.

41. Harmon Killebrew was one of only two Twins to homer into the second deck at Metropolitan Stadium. Who was the other player?

42. Name the former Minnesota Viking running back who starred as a cop on *Hill Street Blues*.

43. Name the Austin, Minnesota, native who went on to fame as an NFL coach and broadcaster.

44. Name the Gustavus Adolphus football player who won the National Football League's "Mr. Irrelevant Award" and the "Lowsman Trophy" for being the last player taken in the 2003 NFL draft.

45. Who was batting a lusty .477 in thirty-six games when he was called from the Minneapolis Millers to play for the parent New York Giants in 1951?

46. Name the Gopher basketball player who was the first player taken in the 1978 National Basketball Association draft.

47. What Minnesota college set a record by losing fifty consecutive football games?

48. How many sacrifice bunts did Harmon Killebrew have in his major league baseball career?

49. What former Minnesota governor starred for the University of Minnesota hockey team?

50. When the real grass was removed from Memorial Stadium at the University of Minnesota, it was replaced with what product from the Minnesota-based 3M Company?

51. When Bill Musselman became the University of Minnesota basketball coach, he replaced a man who held the job for one day before changing his mind. Who was that man?

52. Name the Minneapolis North High School basketball player who went on to lead his Connecticut team to the NCAA National Championship.

53. Minnesota and Wisconsin play each year for Paul Bunyan's Axe. Before that they played for a different trophy. What was that earlier trophy?

54. What former Laker was known as the "Kangaroo Kid?"

55. What did Jack Buck tell viewers after Kirby Puckett's sixth-game walk-off home run in the 1991 World Series?

56. In what league did the Minnesota Fighting Saints compete?

57. What great Gopher receiver and New Prague basketball star share the same first and last names?

58. Cesar Tovar in 1968 played all nine positions in the same game. As a pitcher, what future Hall of Famer did he strike out?

59. What former University of Minnesota football player led the American Football League in scoring every year between 1963 and 1967?

60. Chuck Foreman was the Vikings' second NFL Rookie of the Year. Ten years earlier, a receiver from Northwestern won that honor. Who was he?

61. Ahmad Rashad was one of the great receivers in Minnesota Vikings history. He was obtained in a trade from Seattle for what other Viking "legend"?

62. In what Minnesota town is the U.S. Hockey Hall of Fame located?

63. Name the rookie Minnesota Twins pitcher who, in his major league debut on July 4, 1973, attracted a record crowd of 45,890 fans to Metropolitan Stadium.

64. Which Minnesota Twins player did then manager Billy Martin knock out in a fight outside a Detroit restaurant in 1969?

65. Name the Minnesota North Star who died from a head injury received in a game.

66. What former University of Minnesota football All-American went on to coach his team to the longest winning streak in major college football?

67. What Minnesota woman teamed with Darlene Hard to win the U.S. Lawn Tennis Association (USLTA) doubles event in the mid 1950s?

68. Name the legendary professional golfer whose career began at Minneapolis Washburn High School.

69. Bobby Jones won a leg of golf's legendary Grand Slam in 1930 at what Twin Cities golf course?

70. What Minnesota boxer represented the United States as a heavyweight at the 1972 Munich Olympic Games?

71. What is the name of the football team that represented the city of Duluth in professional football ranks?

72. Name the Minnesota Twin who became a popular write-in candidate for Homecoming Queen at the University of Minnesota in the 1970s.

73. Who was the Minnesota Viking who once introduced himself by saying, "I play third string center for the Minnesota Vikings behind Mick Tingelhoff and Mick Tingelhoff hurt"?

74. Who was the only Minnesota Twins manager to once play for both the St. Paul Saints and the Minneapolis Millers?

75. The only player to ever pinch-hit for Ted Williams also played briefly for the Minnesota Twins. Name him.

76. Who coached Hamline to three national basketball championships between 1942 and 1952?

77. The Boston Red Sox became the last major league baseball team to integrate their lineup when they called up what player from the Minneapolis Millers?

78. Name the only player in the history of the Minnesota Twins whose last name is a perfect palindrome—spelled the same forward and backward.

79. Who is the all-time rushing leader in the history of University of Minnesota football?

80. Name the Warroad, Minnesota, native whose professional hockey career was cut short by a serious eye injury.

81. Name the former Gopher football player who is the only person in modern professional football history to both make an interception and throw for an interception in the same game?

82. St. John's John Gagliardi is the winningest coach in college football history. Perhaps his biggest coaching victory came in 1963 when his team defeated what program for the NAIA national championship?

83. A North America Soccer League record crowd of 46,164 turned out to see the Minnesota Kicks play the New York Cosmos in 1976. Most of the crowd was there to see the star of the Cosmos. Who was he?

84. The Minnesota Twins have had thirteen different twenty-game winners in team history. Two of them are native Minnesotans. Name them.

85. This Native American pitcher, born on Minnesota's

White Earth Reservation in 1883, went on to win 212 major league games and was elected to the Baseball Hall of Fame in 1953. Who was he?

86. Name the woman who made baseball history when she pitched for the St. Paul Saints in 1997.

87. Name the Hamline great who played major league baseball for the Brooklyn Dodgers and professional basketball with the Minneapolis Lakers.

88. One of the greatest female hockey players in U.S. history first gained attention as the catcher for the Brooklyn Center team in the 1994 Little League World Series. Name her.

89. Name the great running back of the 1940s who won the Little Brown Jug as both a Minnesota Gopher and a Michigan Wolverine.

90. In the movie *Field of Dreams*, Kevin Costner and James Earl Jones drive to northern Minnesota to find a man who appeared in a single major league baseball game and never got an official at-bat. What is the name of this real-life Chisholm doctor?

91. This former Gopher hockey player was named MVP in the 2003 Frozen Four and in 2006–07 led the entire National Hockey League in the Plus/Minus category. Who is he?

92.   This man was the first-round choice of the Minnesota Vikings in the 1983 college football draft. He finished his professional sports career as an outfielder with the New York Mets. Who is he?

93.   A Roseau, Minnesota, native, this man is the only person ever to play in the Minnesota State Hockey Tournament, the NCAA Hockey Tournament, the Olympic Games Championship, and the Stanley Cup finals. Who is he?

94.   At the end of the movie *Miracle* is a dedication that reads, "He never saw it. He lived it." To whom is the movie dedicated?

95.   This Minnesotan is generally acknowledged to be the "father of waterskiing." Name him.

96.   In 1976, this Lutsen, Minnesota, native became the first American-born skier to win the World Cup downhill event. Who is she?

97.   This Anoka woman was the goaltender for the U.S. Women's soccer team that won a gold medal in the 1996 Olympic Games and the World Cup three years later. Her name?

98.   As a linebacker, he was one of the greatest tacklers in Gopher football history. A successful options trader, he is today one of the hosts of CNBC's *Fast Money*. Who is this son of another famous Minnesotan?

99. Under what name is Rudolf Walter Wanderone Jr. better known?

100. This one will keep you up nights. There are a dozen last names of U.S. presidents that have been shared by members of the Minnesota Twins in the team's history. How many of the twelve can you name?

Trivia Answers

1. Cookie Lavagetto

2. Harry

3. Twins-O-Gram

4. Rodney Cline Carew

5. Edgerton

6. Sandy Koufax

7. Tennis

8. Steve Cristoff

9. Greg LeMond

10. Bernie Bierman

11. Jack Morris

12. Askov

13. Roy Campanella

14. Dave Winfield

15. Pete Rose

16. Jim Marshall

17. Johnny Lattner

18. Moose

19. Dan Patch

20. Jack Armstrong

21. Bernie Allen

22. Connie Hawkins

23. Harmon Killebrew

24. George Shaw

25. Kent Kitzman

26. Marion Barber II and Marion Barber III

27. New York Mills

28. Tom Lehman

29. The Eagles

30. Winning

31. Eric Magdanz and Ollie Shannon

32. Marion Gaborik

33. Dave Hill

34. Lindsay Whelan

35. Andy MacPhail

36. Randy Breuer

37. Norm Green

38. Chris Weinke

39. Charlie Sanders

40. Brock Lesnar

41. Bobby Darwin

42. Ed Marinaro

43. John Madden

44. Ryan Haug

45. Willie Mays

46. Mychal Thompson

47. Macalester

48. Zero

49. Wendy Anderson

50. Tartan Turf

51. Calvin Luther

52. Khalid El-Amin

53. The Slab of Bacon

54. Jim Pollard

55. "And we'll see you tomorrow night."

56. World Hockey Association

57. Ron Johnson

58. Reggie Jackson

59. Gino Cappelletti

60. Paul Flatley

61. Bob Lurtsema

62. Eveleth

63. Eddie Bane

64. Dave Boswell

65. Bill Masterson

66. Bud Wilkinson

67. Jeanne Arth

68. Patty Berg

69. Interlachen Country Club

70. Duane Bobick

71. Eskimos

72. Bombo Rivera

73. Godfrey Zaunbrecher

74. Gene Mauch

75. Carroll Hardy

76. Joe Hutton

77. Pumpsie Green

78. Mark Salas

79. Darrell Thompson

80. Henry Boucha

81. Tony Dungy

82. Prairie View A&M

83. Pele

84. Dave Goltz and Jerry Koosman

85. Chief Bender

86. Ila Borders

87. Howie Schultz

88. Krissy Wendell

89. Bill Daley

90. Moonlight Graham

91. Thomas Vanek

92. D. J. Dozier

93. Neal Broten

94. Herb Brooks

95. Ralph Samuelson

96. Cindy Nelson

97. Brianna Scurry

98. Pete Najarian

99. Minnesota Fats

100. Washington, Adams, Jackson, Harrison, Buchanan, Lincoln, Johnson, Grant, Wilson, Nixon, Ford, and Bush

Acknowledgments

This book would not have happened without the generous assistance of so many people. Here is a brief list, with apologies to those whose contributions I'll remember in the middle of a night after the book has gone to press.

Thanks first to my wife, Linda, who has heard all these stories so many times that she has shorthand titles for virtually all of them. She was beside me when I needed someone to chart turnovers and rebounds in Mexico City, and she was always the one to suggest that I return to the keyboard when the urge to golf was stronger than the urge to meet a deadline.

Thanks to my three editors who read every word of the manuscript and made great suggestions for elaboration and improvement. My sister, Judy Schell, taught me how to read and write when I was four, and she was there again for me decades later when I needed a proofreader. Erik, my older son and the editor and publisher at Paizo Publications, kept after me for years to write a book. He's done fifteen of his own, and he constantly challenged me to flesh out my brief stories into well-rounded tales. He has served as editor of both *Dungeon* and *Dragon* magazines, and his books are pretty much required reading for D&D enthusiasts.

Our younger son, Kirk, who also writes on a variety of topics relating to nature and the outdoors, provided solid detail on a number of the chapters where he was either a witness or a participant. He also kept me modest with observations such as, "Dad, I see you're already being discounted on Amazon.com. You'll probably be a closeout before you're actually in print."

The first time I met Josh Leventhal at Voyageur Press I knew he'd be a perfect person to serve as the official editor of this book. Baseball reference books, some of which he's written, line his shelves, and a basketball card is neatly tacked to his office wall. His suggestions for how the book should flow, combined with his skillful editing, made for a much better final product.

This is my third book, and any time that I've needed research done at the Minnesota Historical Society, I have been able to count on my longtime friend from the *Minnesota Daily* days, Joe O'Connell, and his friend, Rich Arpi. Nobody knows those files any better. I also want to thank my assistant, Judy Krause, for teaching me all kinds of tricks with my computer, such as how to turn assorted pieces of copy into one continuous document.

I want to thank the *Star Tribune* for permission to reprint several articles that I wrote during the five years I was a reporter there, and WCCO Radio for taking a chance on me more than twenty-five years ago.

Finally, I want to thank Sid Hartman, who provided much of the rich content of this book and whose friendship I have valued for so many years.

Index

Beyond the Sports huddle

33500011125457   sl